Florida A&M University, Tallahassee
Florida Atlantic University, Boca Raton
Florida Gulf Coast University, Ft. Myers
Florida International University, Miami
Florida State University, Tallahassee
University of Central Florida, Orlando
University of Florida, Gainesville
University of North Florida, Jacksonville
University of South Florida, Tampa
University of West Florida, Pensacola

José Martí and U.S. Writers

Anne Fountain

Foreword by Roberto Fernández Retamar

University Press of Florida

Gainesville · Tallahassee · Tampa · Boca Raton
Pensacola · Orlando · Miami · Jacksonville · Ft. Myers

08 07 06 05 04 03   6 5 4 3 2 1

Library of Congress Cataloging-in-Publication Data
Fountain, Anne Owen, 1946–
José Martí and U.S. writers / Anne Fountain; foreword by Roberto
Fernández Retamar.
p. cm.
Includes bibliographical references and index.
ISBN 0-8130-2617-2 (cloth: alk. paper)
1. Martí, José, 1853–1895—Knowledge—American literature.
2. American literature—19th century—Criticism and interpretation.
I. Title.
PQ7389.M2 Z5657 2003
861'.5—dc21 2002075082

The University Press of Florida is the scholarly publishing
agency for the State University System of Florida, comprising
Florida A&M University, Florida Atlantic University, Florida Gulf
Coast University, Florida International University, Florida State
University, University of Central Florida, University of Florida,
University of North Florida, University of South Florida, and
University of West Florida.

University Press of Florida
15 Northwest 15th Street
Gainesville, FL 32611–2079
http://www.upf.com

To Mike

Contents

Photographs

Foreword

José Martí would never have agreed with the concept, now popular again, that civilizations are ever doomed to clash with each other. In 1894, using reasoning that harks back to the time of the Stoics if not before, he claimed categorically that "to speak of nationhood is to speak of humanity." In the upheavals of his own life, he had come to understand that civilizations can and should sustain each other. Thus he labeled the part of our planet where he happened to have been born, and to which he dedicated his life, "Our Mestizo America." Bearing this in mind, it is reasonable to assume that he would have enthusiastically welcomed the multiculturalism currently in vogue in the United States. Martí's relationship with the United States, where he lived in exile for some fifteen years, is enduring proof of this.

However, Martí's intimate and complex relationship with the United States has not yet been adequately studied. At the beginning of this book, Anne Fountain characterizes that relationship succinctly when she says that Martí's "whole interpretation of the United States" was "a largely negative view of politics and politicians tempered by an enthusiastic embrace of poets and poetry." The great poet Juan Ramón Jiménez, an authoritative spokesman for his era, wrote that "Spain and Spanish America were deeply indebted to [Martí] for opening up their access to U.S. poetry." Hence the importance of this study. Although some of Fountain's compatriots, as well as some Latin American scholars, have pointed out Martí's connections to such writers and thinkers as Emerson, Longfellow, Whitman, or Twain, this study is the first to consider in their entirety the numerous perceptive insights of Martí into U.S. culture. For this reason, her book is especially valuable.

Years ago, I had the pleasure of reading a photocopy of the author's Ph.D. dissertation, "José Martí and North American Authors," presented to Columbia University in New York in 1973. Since then, I have followed closely her various publications on this important aspect of Martí's work. Her thesis and those other publications have now led to the book in the reader's hands. It is an indisputably useful book, which will enhance our comprehension of José Martí's fascinating personality even as it contributes to our knowledge of ourselves as North Americans and Latin Americans, clears away needless misunderstandings, and brings us closer on the basis of our shared humanity.

Roberto Fernández Retamar
Havana, December 25, 2001
Translated by Mary G. Berg, Harvard University

Preface

José Martí died in 1895 while charging a Spanish artillery position during Cuba's war for independence. The money, arms, and volunteers he raised to carry on the struggle against Spain made him Cuba's most exalted patriot and martyr for the cause of independence. Previously Martí had spent nearly fifteen years in the United States, in political exile and as a struggling journalist. His bibliography is huge, as is the body of works about him: OCLC's world catalog lists 1,030 titles by Martí and more than 750 titles about him.

One aspect of Martí's U.S. period that for the most part has eluded researchers—especially those writing in English—is his profound fascination with American letters. Martí read avidly from the nineteenth-century American bookshelf, with an uncommon thirst for penetrating the soul of his temporary homeland. His myriad works on American authors, mostly published in Spanish for his Latin American readers, ran the gamut from Ralph Waldo Emerson to Henry James. These essays and comments conveyed deep respect for the society that could produce such writers, but they also helped shape a portrait of America the colossus, the Caliban, the emerging world power. Understanding Martí's literary criticism, therefore, is central to grasping his whole interpretation of the United States—a largely negative view of politics and politicians tempered by an enthusiastic embrace of poets and poetry.

Some scholars who have interpreted Martí's critical opus have assumed that he was simply a journeyman writer who absorbed, analyzed, and presented his subjects to his readership. Yet a close examination of the total production—essays, letters, notes, and translations—together with careful comparison with the English originals, reveals that Martí consciously sought to depict American literary life for his Spanish

American readers, and did so based on thorough knowledge and informed reading.

This study organizes, by author, Martí's writing about forty U.S. authors. It offers full-chapter treatments of Emerson, Whitman, and Longfellow, and groups dozens of other writers into separate chapters on Martí and Romantic writers and Martí and authors associated with Realism.

The book provides a complete examination of Martí's multiple connections with U.S. literature, yet it is much more than a catalogue of writers. It tells which authors Martí favored, gives the reasons for his selections, indicates his degree of affinity with individual writers, and when feasible locates his critique within the context of American literary criticism. It shows how his writing about U.S. authors revealed aesthetic preferences and notions about the function of literature. In addition, it sheds new light on Martí's importance as a translator of American literature by identifying and analyzing translated material in his essays and notes. This treatment of Martí and U.S. literature is based on an exhaustive reading of his *Obras Completas* and on thorough research about the U.S. authors he interpreted for his Spanish-speaking readers.

In completing this research and writing, I gratefully acknowledge the support and encouragement of colleagues at the Centro de Estudios Martianos (Center for Martí Studies) in Havana and the leave time granted by Peace College.

1

The Making of a Martyr

José Martí, one of Latin America's foremost writers and Cuba's national hero, was born in Havana on January 28, 1853, and died on May 19, 1895, at Dos Ríos in the eastern part of the island, a martyr to the cause that was central to his life, Cuban independence. He was only forty-two when he died, but he had lived a life of great intensity and productivity. Martí lived in exile in various countries and spent nearly fifteen years in the United States, where he wrote articles about North America for Spanish American readers and where he became familiar with the lives and works of U.S. authors.

Cuba still belonged to Spain when Martí was born. His father, Mariano Martí, was an artilleryman from Valencia and his mother, Leonor Pérez, a native of the Canary Islands. His beginnings were humble and the house where he was born—now a museum dedicated to his memory—was modest. Martí was their first child and only son.

Martí began his education in a local school. His ability and intellect soon indicated a need for greater challenge, however, and at age ten Martí began studies at San Ancleto, a highly regarded school where he received classes in English and where he met Fermín Valdés Domínguez, who was to become a lifelong friend. When he was twelve, Martí moved to the Escuela Superior Municipal de Varones, a city high school for boys, whose director, Rafael María de Mendive, proved to be an intellectual mentor and inspiration for Martí. Mendive, a progressive educator and poet, guided Martí in ways that complemented the honest but simple qualities of Mariano Martí, and his influence on Martí was profound—both in literature and in politics. He introduced Martí to the serious study of literature, including literature in English, and heightened the young man's appreciation of drama. Mendive also provided the example of poet, playwright, magazine publisher, and translator and instilled in his students a deep yearning for Cuban independence from the mother country. These ideas took especially deep root in José Martí.

In the Cuba of Martí's childhood and youth, both slavery and the slave trade from Africa continued. As a boy of ten Martí spent time with his father in Hanábana, not far from Havana, and there witnessed a cruel *bocabajo* or flogging, the memory of which made his cheeks flush with shame. References in Martí's notes indicate that from that time forward he was determined to redress this wrong. Another crucial factor during Martí's life was the political ascendancy of the United States and its increasing interest and influence in Latin America. Several constituencies in the United States, including those in the pre–Civil War slaveholding states, advocated the acquisition of Cuba as an additional territory or as another "slave state," and various attempts were made to purchase Cuba from the mother country. Thus the Cuba that formed José Martí's life was framed by Cuban desire for freedom from Spain, fear of U.S. imperialism toward Cuba, and the continuing tragedy of slavery. All of these elements are present in his writing.

In 1868, Cuban rebels wishing to throw off the Spanish yoke sounded the "grito de Yara," a cry for independence that ushered in the Ten Years' War by Cuban guerrillas against the forces of Spain. Martí, quite naturally in sympathy with the rebels, contributed articles to two newspapers that he helped to found in 1869, *El Diablo Cojuelo* (The Limping Devil) and *La Patria Libre* (The Free Fatherland). Although neither paper survived more than a single issue, they clearly established the extent of young Martí's political commitment and his vision of Cuba's options: either "Yara" or "Madrid," that is, complete independence or a continuation of the colonial status. Later in the same year, Martí was seized by Spanish authorities because he had cosigned a letter accusing a schoolmate of supporting Spain. While Martí and Fermín Valdés Domínguez had both signed the letter, Martí assumed the responsibility and took the punishment: six years at hard labor, later commuted to exile in Spain. Martí served six months of the original sentence toiling under a tropical sun in the quarries of San Lázaro. He wore leg irons and experienced the abuses and privations of Spanish political imprisonment. The half year of forced labor left physical as well as emotional marks and bolstered his determination to see Cuba free from colonial tyranny.

Exile in Spain lasted from 1871 to 1874. Martí earned degrees in law and in philosophy and letters, assumed an active role in Cuban political circles, and supported himself through private classes and translations from English. In Zaragoza, in the province of Aragon, he experienced relative tranquility, formed friendships, learned to appreciate the valor and integrity of the Spanish people—as opposed to the government and politicians—and fell in love. The rewarding memories of Zaragoza are recalled in one of his autobiographical poems, number VII of *Versos sencillos* (Simple Verses),[1] as one of the happiest times in his life. In 1874 Martí left Spain and traveled through France to England. In Paris he met Victor Hugo and received a copy of Hugo's pamphlet *Mes Fils* (My Sons, 1874), a work he translated into Spanish and published the next year and one that reinforced the Cuban author's interest in both the theory and the practice of literary translation. From England, Martí booked passage on a steamer and headed to Mexico, where his family had relocated. After landing at Veracruz, Martí traveled by rail to Mexico City. In Mexico he was greeted by both sorrow and promise: he learned of the death of his sister Ana, but he also made the acquaintance of a young Mexican, Manuel Mercado, who became one of his most trusted friends.

In Mexico, Martí contributed newspaper articles, theatre and art critiques, poetry, and his translation of *Mes Fils* to a Mexican journal, *La Revista Universal*. He also wrote a one-act play with a theme of love, developed several romantic interests, and became engaged to an elegant young Cuban woman from a wealthy family, Carmen Zayas Bazán. Also while in Mexico, Martí began to conceive of the common patrimony of the Spanish American lands and to view Cuba as part of a greater homeland that he called Nuestra América (Our America). This concept became a theme in his later writing and served as a contrast to the United States.[2]

After a brief trip to Cuba on a Mexican passport, Martí traveled to Guatemala, where he taught courses in languages and literature. Once his teaching position was firmly established, Martí went to Mexico to keep his promise of marriage to Carmen Zayas Bazán, and in January of 1878 he returned with his bride to Guatemala. The return was made sad, however, by the death of María García Granados, a young girl from a distinguished family who had apparently fallen in love with Martí and was heartbroken when he returned a married man. María García Granados, "la niña de Guatemala," later became the subject of one of Martí's best-known poems, number IX of *Versos sencillos*.

In 1878 the Ten Years' War ended, and under a general proviso of pardon it became legally feasible for Martí to return to Cuba. He moved with his wife to Havana and soon began working to promote independence for Cuba. Predictably, Martí found himself arrested and exiled to Spain; in September of 1879 he sailed from Cuba, leaving behind his wife and a baby son, José.

Martí spent little time in Spain; he quickly discovered that Europe provided scant opportunity for political work and few ways to provide for his family. He decided to travel to the United States and undertook an intense study of English. Martí's aim was to work with Cuban immigrants who lived in the United States but maintained loyalty to Cuba. With these plans and options in mind, Martí arrived in New York City in January of 1880.

Far from the palms of his native Cuba and alone in what he was to call the Iron City, Martí felt the absence of his wife and son keenly. He wrote to a friend in Cuba and got help in securing their passage to New York. The arrival of his wife and son in March of 1880 did little to ease Martí's burdens, however. His wife could not understand his commitment to the struggle in Cuba, criticized him for his lesser commitment to assuring the family's future, and, at the end of 1880, chose to return to Cuba, taking their son with her. For the exile who had endured so much, the fact that his wife never shared the convictions central to his life was an enormous personal tragedy. Martí turned for solace to Carmen Miyares de Mantilla, a Venezuelan who ran a boardinghouse in New York, and in "Carmita" he found a true companion and source of comfort. He is presumed to be the father of her daughter María Mantilla, who was in turn the mother of the actor Cesar Romero, who proudly claimed Martí as his grandfather.

In 1881 Martí traveled to Venezuela, where he spent five months teaching and writing and where tender memories of his son produced a book of poems called *Ismaelillo* (Little Ismael), which was published in 1882. In Venezuela he stirred minds and emotions with his oratory and writing, and before he left, the director of a major newspaper in Caracas arranged for him to send articles from New York. The time in Venezuela expanded Martí's horizons in Spanish America and also—through the example of Venezuelan strongman Guzmán Blanco—made him more aware of the unfortunate consequences of *caudillo* rule in the Spanish American lands.

Martí in New York, 1885. Photograph by W. F. Bowers from *Iconografía Martiana*. By permission of the Centro de Estudios Martianos, Havana.

When Martí returned to New York in 1881, he began writing articles for the Venezuelan periodical *La Opinión Nacional*. Before long he was writing for *La Nación* of Buenos Aires and other newspapers in Latin America, and over the next fourteen years in the United States, from 1881 to 1895, Martí became an "epic chronicler" of North American life. His essays about the United States in the 1880s and 1890s represent a detailed description of the social, economic, political, literary, and cultural milieu of an increasingly aggressive and expansionistic nation, one whose eagle came to symbolize, for Martí, imperialist design and deceitful intent. His legitimate fear of U.S. imperialism in regard to Cuba is clearly evinced in many of his works and stands in contrast to his admiration for many elements of American society—especially its men and women of letters.

Martí as a writer covered a range of genres. In addition to producing newspaper articles and keeping up an extensive correspondence, he wrote a serialized novel, composed poetry—*Versos libres* (Free Verses, 1913) and *Versos sencillos* (1891)—and published four issues of a children's magazine, *La Edad de Oro* (The Golden Age, 1889).

Martí's style is difficult to categorize. He was a master of aphorisms—short, memorable lines that convey truth and/or wisdom—and of long and complex sentences. He is considered a major contributor to the Spanish American literary movement known as *modernismo* and has been linked to Latin American consciousness of the modern age and modernity.[3] Through chronicles that combined elements of literary portraiture, dramatic narration, and a dioramic scope, Martí reached an emerging generation of Latin American writers. His poetry offered fresh and astonishing images along with deceptively simple sentiments. As an orator, he exhorted with cascading structure, powerful aphorisms, intense descriptive scenes, and compelling cadences.

Throughout his writing Martí made reference to historical figures and events, alluded to authors, titles, and examples from literature, and noted items of current news and cultural matters. For all these reasons he can be difficult to read and presents enormous challenges to his translators. Many of his allusions are subject to conjecture.

In addition to writing, Martí worked in the United States as a translator, taught evening classes of Spanish, held diplomatic posts for Uruguay, Argentina, and Paraguay, represented Latin American interests at inter-American conferences in the United States, was active in the social and political activities of the Cuban colony, and served as president of the Spanish American Literary Society.

After 1891, nearly all of Martí's activities centered on the goal of Cuban independence. In 1892 he organized the Cuban Revolutionary Party, which included a widespread network of local clubs. He also founded and did most of the writing for *Patria*, the Cuban Revolutionary Party journal. In planning for a new struggle in Cuba, he traveled to the Cuban colonies in Tampa, Key West, and elsewhere and raised both spirits and funds for the Cuban revolution. As a part of the effort, Martí had to bring diverse interests together and to wage a powerful war of words to ensure that the movement would not fail the Cuban people in its aims. He had to counter the interests of military leaders, those content with autonomy (home rule rather than independence for Cuba), and those desiring annexation to the United States.

Then in January of 1895, when all finally seemed ready for the attack on Spanish forces in Cuba, the Cuban revolutionaries were betrayed and the United States confiscated their boats and munitions. Despite this crushing blow, Martí determined to join his compatriots in the struggle and, along with Máximo Gómez, the military leader of the revolution, landed in Cuba in early 1895. Thirty-eight days after the landing, on May 19, 1895, Martí was killed by a volley of fire from Spanish troops.

Martí's life is much like his writing: prolific yet precise; without boundaries, yet bound always to Cuba; with dimensions both public and private. He spoke and wrote three languages (Spanish, English, and French); lived in Cuba, Spain, Mexico, Guatemala, Venezuela, and the United States; was an author, translator, teacher, and diplomat; was known for powerful oratory and intense personal charisma; abhorred slavery and promoted racial harmony; helped Latin Americans to understand the United States and defended the interests of Latin America vis-à-vis the United States; was a faithful friend and a devoted son and father; died heroically in the cause of Cuban freedom; and became the national hero of his beloved fatherland. His writings, both prose and poetry, along with the historical framework of his time and the extraordinary impact of his life, have made him Cuba's most universal figure.

Life in the United States

When Martí, armed with scant resources but large ambitions, an imperfect but adequate command of English, and no sure prospects of employment, arrived in New York in January of 1880, he began nearly fifteen years of life in the United States, a period that produced his major work as a writer and his principal activity as a patriot. He became Spanish America's most discerning chronicler of North America during its Gilded Age, and proved a more adroit and astute interpreter of U.S. life than de Tocqueville or Sarmiento.[1] His columns filled the pages of Spanish American newspapers with vivid accounts and colorful commentary gleaned from both extensive reading and firsthand experience.

From 1880 to 1895 Martí experienced and described a United States that bristled with challenge and change. The tensions following the Civil War, an influx of immigrants, discoveries in science and technology, the expansion of the western frontier, and the covetous gaze cast upon Spanish American lands by the United States, all comprised part of Martí's North America. In addition to recording the drama of major events and the minutiae of daily news, Martí formed impressions of the colossus that became a central part of his sociopolitical thinking. Further, the years in the United States allowed him to plumb issues of race, gender, and nationalism against a backdrop of life in an emerging world power.[2]

Martí, in his introduction to the political sphere, witnessed a climate of both reform and corruption. President Rutherford B. Hayes had lost party loyalty and a chance for a second term by attempting to limit patronage politics—especially in the New York customhouse—and by seeking to curb the New York machine run by Senator Roscoe Conkling. When the 1880 Republican National Convention opened in June, a field of new candidates shared the stage: James G. Blaine, Ulysses S. Grant, and dark horse candidate James A. Garfield. Garfield became the nominee, with Chester A. Arthur as his running mate. Conkling, Blaine, Grant, Garfield, and Arthur all figured in Martí's writing about the United States, and their actions, especially Blaine's, contributed to Martí's interpretation of North American politics.

Martí's political consciousness was honed during his years of exile in the United States and by his growing disillusionment with the unbridled capitalism afflicting American society.[3] Throughout the 1890s and especially after 1892, Martí became very concerned by the impact that U.S. interests in Latin America might have on his plans for Cuban liberation. In 1889 he was an observer at the first Pan-American Conference, in Washington, D.C., and witnessed attempts by U.S. Secretary of State James G. Blaine to control inter-American affairs.[4] In March of that year Martí responded to an editorial, published in the *Philadelphia Manufacturer* and picked up by the *New York Evening Post,* that was disdainful of Cubans ("Do we want Cuba?"). His forceful reply defended Cuba's right to be independent of both the United States and Spain.[5] And by the end of his North American residence Martí contrasted U.S. and Spanish designs on Cuba by asking rhetorically: "Who, in order to escape a scarecrow [Spain], would willingly cast himself into the fires of an oven [the United States]?"[6]

Martí in New York City

Martí became an enthusiastic participant in New York City life. He savored the arts—visiting museums and attending concerts and lectures—and joined the throngs who witnessed parades and celebrations. His sampling of New York included views of the lavish festivities of the wealthy as well as the lives of the poor. From rubbing elbows with the city's citizens, he knew firsthand of urban problems such as housing and public transportation. His contacts with the Spanish American and non-Hispanic communities provided a multifaceted perspective of what New York offered and how her inhabitants fared on a day-to-day basis.

Persons who knew Martí in his New York years described him as a "live wire" who functioned at a nearly frenetic pace.[7] The exile's tasks were many: earning a living, providing for his family, maintaining an extensive correspondence, continuing literary activities, and promoting

Martí with the family of Juan Peoli in Sandy Hill, New York, 1893. Peoli was the uncle of Carmen Miyares de Mantilla and had a summer residence in Sandy Hill, on the Hudson River. Photograph from *Iconografía Martiana.* By permission of the Centro de Estudios Martianos, Havana.

the cause of Cuban independence. He lived at Carmita Miyares's boardinghouse, first in Manhattan and then at its Brooklyn location, and for a brief period secured a rented house for his wife and son. He maintained an office at 120 Front Street in lower Manhattan, translated for the publisher Appleton and Company, was a commercial employee for Lyons and Company, taught classes of Spanish at Central Evening High School, and offered instruction for La Liga Society, an educational center for black Cubans. In addition, he was connected to a network of New York offices and homes through his consular work and friendships.[8]

Martí came to know New York's landmarks and the venues for the city's major events. Both the Brooklyn Bridge (1883) and the Statue of Liberty (1886) were inaugurated while Martí was living in New York, and Cooper Union, Steck Hall, Steinway Hall, Hardman Hall, and other sites for public assembly were integral to his life in the city. In Manhattan, Martí frequented newspaper offices, cultural institutions, hotels, and restaurants. He took the Fulton Ferry between Manhattan and Brooklyn, and walked along Fifth Avenue, Broadway, and countless lesser thoroughfares.[9] Today an impressive statue of Martí on horseback graces Central Park South and makes Martí himself a landmark in a city he knew intimately.

While in New York, Martí also rendered diplomatic service to Uruguay, Paraguay, and Argentina. These appointments boosted his finances, enhanced his contacts, and helped to define his vision of the Spanish American countries as Nuestra América, a cultural and historical unit that stood in contrast to the United States. Moreover, serving as Uruguay's representative at the Inter-American Monetary Commission of 1891, Martí successfully defended the interests of Latin America as a whole in opposing James G. Blaine's attempt to impose bimetallism on the hemisphere. He continued these activities until October of 1891, when he resigned his diplomatic posts to devote himself to the cause of Cuba.

Martí's interlude in upstate New York in August of 1890 has been often overlooked. Wearied by the specter of U.S. domination revealed in the 1889 Pan-American Conference, and under doctor's orders to rest, Martí traveled to the Catskill Mountains. The ambience proved conducive to both repose and reflection and prompted a retrospective of his life—conveyed through poetry. There he composed his *Versos sencillos*, which he introduced to friends in an oral recitation and later published in New York City. The poems of *Versos sencillos* show the influence of American literature—in particular an Emersonian imprint—while conveying the very essence of Martí. They are undoubtedly the works that have made Martí well known around the world.[10]

Although New York City served as Martí's prism for understanding life in the United States, from the beginning he was aware that a comprehensive vision of the country required wider horizons. As early as 1880 he wrote: "The great heart of America cannot be judged by the distorted, morbid passion and ardent desires and anguishes of New York life" (19:114). Martí visited Cape May, Bath Beach, and Newport, and traveled to cities along the eastern seaboard and in the Southeast. As his diplomatic and revolutionary activities increased, he also journeyed to Philadelphia, Washington, Atlanta, New Orleans, Jacksonville, St. Augustine, Tampa, Ocala, and Key West. Travel in Florida, in particular, produced a profound engagement with the Cuban communities located there.

In Tampa, which Martí first visited in 1892, his impact was immediate. Invited by the Ignacio Agramonte Club of Cuban patriots, Martí arrived by train on November 26. On the following days he gave two of his most famous speeches, "Con todos y para el bien de todos" (With all and for the good of all) and "Los pinos nuevos" (The new pines). The power and persuasion of his oratory electrified the tobacco workers, galvanized support for the Cuban Revolution, and gained Martí almost legendary status among his Cuban compatriots in Florida.

In the last three years of Martí's stay in the United States, he focused his efforts on the liberation of Cuba, and his essays and articles depicting North American society for Spanish American periodicals virtually disappeared. Instead, the United States increasingly appeared in his writing as a behemoth that posed a very real danger for Cuba.

Martí as U.S. Chronicler

Martí's decade and a half in the United States and his unique vantage point as outsider allowed him to serve as a cultural interpreter of the United States for Latin Americans. Between 1881 and 1892, Martí wrote hundreds of sketches about U.S. life for more than fifteen different Latin American journals. His essays reached Caracas, Buenos Aires, and other parts of Spanish America only days after their composition, providing *caraqueños, porteños,* and those from other cities with timely portrayals of North American scenes.[11] For his spiritual homeland, Nuestra América, Martí depicted his home in exile with an energy that matched the pace of the energy-driven colossus. In turn, Spanish American response to Martí as an interpreter of the United States was enthusiastic.

American life played an important role in Martí's opus. The majority of the articles specifically about the United States take up five of the twenty-eight volumes of his *Obras Completas,* under the headings "North American Scenes" and "North Americans." Additional references are found throughout his writing.

Martí sent his essays about U.S. life to journals in many parts of the hemisphere. The two newspapers that published most of his commentaries were *La Opinión Nacional* of Caracas and *La Nación* of Buenos Aires. From 1881 to 1882, Martí contributed articles and a column called "Sección Constante" to the Caracas paper, and from 1882 to 1891 he wrote for *La Nación.*

Between 1881 and 1892 he sold articles to *La Pluma* of Bogotá, *La República* of Honduras, *La Opinión Pública* of Montevideo, *El Partido Liberal* of Mexico, *El Sudamericano* of Buenos Aires, *La Revista Azul* of Mexico, and *El Almendares* of Havana. He also contributed to New York periodicals: *El Economista Americano, La América, El Avisador Cubano, El Avisador Hispano Americano, La Juventud, El Porvenir,* and *La Revista Ilustrada.*

Martí's correspondence for various newspapers during the 1880s dealt with other topics as well. He was a conscientious reporter of European scenes for the citizens of Nuestra América, taking advantage of New York's timeliness in reporting European events thanks to the transatlantic cable (20:140–41). Much of what Martí wrote concerned Latin America, and nearly two of the twenty-eight volumes of his *Obras Completas* are devoted to European themes. From 1881 to 1882, for example, Martí sent nearly sixty commentaries or news stories about Europe to the Caracas newspaper *La Opinión Nacional.* Additionally, he contributed articles about European art and literature to newspapers in Spanish America and the United States. Martí's prose pieces on European themes provided insight, but they lacked the immediacy and intensity of his reporting on North America.

Martí brought broad and varied experience to his labors as correspondent in the United States. As a young man in Cuba, he had penned *El Diablo Cojuelo* (The Limping Devil), a patriotic work; in exile in Spain he continued to write polemical articles. In Mexico, where he joined his family in 1875, Martí had found an expanded environment for his talents. He wrote for *El Federalista* and contributed poetry, theatre and art reviews, commentary, editorials, and a Victor Hugo memoir in translation to *La Revista Universal.* In Mexico he also began to employ U.S. sources for his writing. Martí defended Cuban interests in columns for *La Revista Universal* to counter charges made by Mexican newspapers that were sympathetic to Spain. In doing so, he referenced the *Times,* the *Picayune,* and the *Bulletin,* all of New Orleans.[12] As early as 1875, Martí mentioned taking information from foreign journals, including newspapers from New York (1:119–40).

Martí's first writing assignment in the United States was for the *Hour,* a New York weekly. There he published brief reviews of art and three long articles titled "Impressions of America by a very fresh Spaniard." In July, August, and October 1880, these early observations about life in the

United States were printed, without correction or editing, in a readable, albeit imperfect, English.[13] Martí also collaborated on articles written in French and translated into English for the *Sun*, whose director, Charles A. Dana, was a friend to Cubans in exile.[14]

Martí's "Impressions of America" described the hustle and bustle of city life, the pervasive interest in material well-being, and the soundness of the American work ethic. He also wrote with fascination on the ways of American women, attributing to them a virile pace and a lamentable love of riches. He longed for a smile and a feminine manner that could stir his emotions, declaring: "I have not found in New York my two lovely eyes!" (19:113). He concluded with observations about his difficulty in understanding spoken English and a lament about the poor and downtrodden in the city (19:101–26).

After his early jobs for newspapers in New York, Martí spent five months in Venezuela. There he continued to write and published a magazine called *La Revista Venezolana*. When he returned to New York in the summer of 1881 with an assignment to write articles from New York for the Caracas paper *La Opinión Nacional*, Martí was launched on a long and successful career as reader and interpreter of American life for Latin Americans.

As an observer of the United States in the 1880s, Martí drew on three main sources. First, he used his personal observations as a resident who could read, write, speak, and understand the language. His knowledge of English improved over the years, became thorough and discerning, and earned him entrée in a variety of circumstances. Second, Martí used texts and reference works in the preparation of his articles, as revealed in a letter to his lifelong friend Manuel Mercado (20:126). Third, he read U.S. and European newspapers available in New York. Among his sources from Europe, Martí referenced *Le Figaro* of Paris, the *London Post*, the *London Evening Standard*, and the *Revue des Deux Mondes*. From the United States, he cited New York newspapers such as the *Herald* (the source he referred to most frequently), the *Sun*, the *Tribune*, the *World*, and the *Times*. He also mentioned papers in Washington, Atlanta, Philadelphia, and other cities. For magazines, Martí turned to *Harper's Weekly, Harper's New Monthly*, the *Century* (formerly *Scribner's*), the *North American Review*, and *Popular Science Monthly*. He even proposed in an 1884 article in *La América* to write a monthly report on three of these journals. Additionally, Martí cited specialized publications like the *Journal of Commerce,* the *Scientific American,* and the *Magazine of American History.*

Martí believed a writer should be broadly informed "about everything from the heavens above to the tiniest microbe and from Omar Khayyam to Pasteur" (10:235), and both newspapers and magazines served as sources for this purpose. In an 1883 article for readers in Buenos Aires, Martí gave a vivid picture of the journalist at work: "There before me, in long stands of small type that I spread out and review, are the events of the month taking shape" (9:413). In a comment of 1884 Martí wrote that "reading a good magazine is like reading dozens of good books" (13:437).

Martí was both panoramic and precise as a chronicler of the United States. He conveyed the colossal scale of an ambitious and growing nation and portrayed the dynamism of her society. In 1883 he wrote: "Life in Venice is a gondola; in Paris, a golden carriage; in Madrid, a bouquet of flowers; in New York, a locomotive going full speed with furiously puffing smoke" (9:443). In the same piece Martí said of the human condition, "Here men do not die, they collapse: they are not organisms that waste away, but instead fall, like Icarus" (9:443).

The first articles Martí sent to *La Opinión Nacional,* in the fall of 1881, described the assassination attempt on President Garfield, the trial of the assassin, and the president's eventual death. These events led Martí into the thicket of American politics and to a cohort of politicians whom he profiled for his readers. He wrote of the presidents who followed Garfield—Arthur, Cleveland, and Harrison—and paid tribute to Grant on the occasion of his death and burial in New York. Martí lived in the United States during a succession of mediocre presidents. Nonetheless he was aware that the nation was capable of producing noble political leaders, and he wrote with appreciation of Franklin, Washington, and Lincoln. He held Lincoln in special regard, remembering from boyhood the sorrow felt in Havana at the news of Lincoln's assassination. Martí also praised Lincoln in one of his most famous remarks about the United States. Contrasting the great American president with an opportunistic journalist who sought to provoke an incident between the United States and Mexico, Martí wrote: "We love the land of Lincoln, as much as we fear the country of Cutting" (1:237).

Presidents, vice presidents, cabinet members, and members of Congress all assembled on the stage of Martí's theatre of American political life. Martí drew sympathetic portraits of Tilden, for his high-minded conduct in the election fraud of 1877, and of Cleveland, for integrity in appointments to public office (10:244). On the other hand, he was suspicious and fearful of the imperialistic mind-set and machinations of James G. Blaine, even as he conceded that Blaine was a skillful statesman.

Martí's readers learned of the American political system in its multiple facets: caucuses, conventions, campaigns, and elections. Through Martí's words they witnessed a presidential inauguration—and the first-ever marriage of an American president in the White House, when Grover Cleveland and Frances Folsom exchanged vows in 1886 (10:480–83).[15] They also discovered that democracy in the United States had problems: voter ignorance, vote buying in beer halls, election fraud, corruption among public officials, scandal at many levels, and the "spoils system" (10:279–80). They learned that in New York the Tammany Hall machine committed an array of political abuses. Although Martí described many negative aspects of the American political scene, he also praised what was positive and showed examples of fair procedures and honesty at the polls (9:107).

Throughout his writing about the United States, Martí imparted information about political questions and debates. He discussed trade issues and explained why he was opposed to the protective tariff. He wrote about immigration policies, especially in regard to the Chinese, about mistreatment of the American Indians, and about a suitable strategy for dealing with the post–Civil War South. He also sketched the background and general philosophies of the two major political parties in the United States.

In the course of writing about America, Martí studied the spectrum of prominent men: scientists, entrepreneurs, scalawags, generals, politicians, orators, clergymen, and philanthropists.[16] In some cases he dedicated entire articles to individuals; in other cases a name appeared again and again throughout his works.

José Martí lived in the United States during the Gilded Age, when wealth and the wealthy were particularly ostentatious. He described in detail the extravagant lifestyles, gala social events, and palatial homes enjoyed by the rich, and noted the phenomenon of monied Americans marrying titled Europeans (13:32–33). As observer and critic of American ways, Martí was repulsed by the ruthlessness of the robber barons. He detested the speculators who gambled with the nation's interests, and he deplored the idea of making money as an end in itself. In fact, Martí's major criticism of Americans was their excessive emphasis on money and material acquisitions (10:63). At the same time, Martí did not consider wealth per se a sin and appreciated that the nation that tolerated a selfish financier like Jay Gould could also produce a benevolent philanthropist like Peter Cooper.

Martí portrayed the great labor struggles of the times. He exposed injustices suffered by workers and described the rise and growth of unions such as the Knights of Labor. He attended workers' parades and wrote of the beginning of the Labor Day tradition in September (10:309). Martí's accounts covered clashes between police and workers, and he took great interest in the events of the Haymarket riot in Chicago—one of the most memorable labor conflicts of the era. In various articles, Martí described the social turmoil surrounding the workers, the horror of the explosives that killed several policemen, and the anguish and uncertainty of the trial, in which seven anarchists were found guilty and sentenced to be hanged (11:55–61, 333–56). In general Martí was sympathetic to organized labor. He disagreed strongly, however, when the Knights of Labor gave support to white miners on strike who waged a campaign of terror against the Chinese workers hired to replace them (10:306–7).

New York, a gateway for immigrants and a shelter for the "huddled masses" from many lands, was a perfect vantage point for Martí's treatment of America's national and ethnic diversity.[17] His narratives described the influx of Irish, German, Italian, Scandinavian, Jewish, and Chinese immigrants, and he detailed the problems as well as the prospects faced by the newcomers. As a foreign-born resident, Martí was keenly aware of the differing customs that immigrants brought and of the diverse contributions they made to American life (12:64–83).

Martí saw Americans as joiners: crusaders, moralizers, campaigners, and conventioneers. He wrote about the temperance movement, suffragettes, labor drives, and the rise of socialism. His essays explained the work of charities, depicted causes on behalf of the poor, and described gatherings of the clergy. He also gave his readers a sense of the numerous assemblies that took place, from a convention of the American Association for the Advancement of Science to a meeting of bankers (12:336–40).

A signal theme for Martí, whether writing about Cuba, the United States, or any other country, was respect for mankind—regardless of race.[18] Martí had witnessed the cruelty of bondage in Cuba, lamented the death of Lincoln, who symbolized the end of slavery in the United States, and admired America's abolitionists. His writing reflected this focus and underscored his concern for race relations. In an 1885 article, Martí discussed the nation's attempts to heal the wounds caused by the Civil War and voiced cautious optimism about black-white relations (10:316). Later writing painted a different picture, however, showing the economic plight of blacks in the South, raids on black communities, and lynchings (11:237–38). He dedicated a brief article to the black orator Henry Garnet, and made more than a dozen references to abolition hero Frederick Douglass, who served as U.S. ambassador to Haiti.

Martí wanted his readers to know about Native Americans in the United States—especially their mistreatment at the hands of scheming government agents, and their miserable life on the reservations. He wrote of the various tribes, named prominent chiefs such as Red Cloud, and described the role of the Indians in "Wild West" spectacles presented in New York (11:33–35). He praised efforts at reform, including the establishment of Indian schools, and took special interest in author Helen Hunt Jackson because of her dedication to helping the Indians.

Religion and religious leaders both Protestant and Catholic were also subjects of Martí's essays about U.S. life. Among these, Henry Ward Beecher received special attention. Martí also noted the distinctive facets of Protestant evangelism: revivals, summer church camps, and faith healing. Martí linked the growth in Catholicism in the United States to the increase in European immigrants from Catholic countries and wrote about the construction of St. Patrick's Cathedral in New York as a consequence of this growth. A twelve-page essay focused on the Father McGlynn controversy, a conflict between an activist priest and the Catholic hierarchy that engulfed New York in 1887. In his initial article and continuing comments about the case, Martí contrasted the good heart and noble instincts of Father McGlynn with the rigidity of church dogma, and the Cuban writer aligned himself squarely with the humble priest. This writing also afforded Martí the opportunity to champion concern for the poor and to question whether Catholic doctrine could function effectively in a free nation (11:139).

Although Martí filled columns with descriptions of serious problems and the darker side of democracy, his gaze extended to lighter moments and festive events as well. His American scenes included centennial celebrations, parades, exhibitions, and holiday traditions, and his readers followed the inaugurations of the Brooklyn Bridge completion and the Statue of Liberty.

Sport and spectacle formed another facet of the America described by Martí. His reports covered cattle fairs and flower shows, a prizefight and a walking marathon. He wrote about university sports such as rowing and football, and noted the winter recreations of skating and sleighing.

Cultural life was an indispensable part of the image of America that Martí created for his readers, and New York's array of galleries, museums, and lecture halls provided a rich setting. Opera, drama, public discourse, and art shows all figured in Martí's writing, and he referred frequently to stage personalities. He was active in literary circles, engaged in declamations, and read avidly. His own production included numerous book reviews, along with essays for the press, an extensive correspondence—much of it related to literature—and his poetry, fiction, children's literature, and translations.

In the realm of education, Martí presented a panoramic view. He wrote approvingly of nearly all the Ivy League universities, mentioning Columbia frequently and writing of Cornell with special favor. He touched on the public schools by noting their problems: overcrowding, an emphasis on rote learning rather than discovery, and a lack of empathy on the part of the teachers. He also highlighted the virtues of Chautauqua, America's "university of the poor."

From the very beginning, women in America fascinated Martí. He wrote about them as supporters of cultural events, as members of the labor force, and as city dwellers who often had to fend for themselves. He wrote sympathetically of Susan B. Anthony and the suffragette movement. Still, he believed that a woman's primary role was in the home. He observed that newspapers were developing women's sections, and he reported on women at the ballot box. Most American women were too assertive for Martí's taste, but he admired their industry and appreciated their social consciousness.

Some of Martí's best pieces about North American life applied his literary talent to describing the awesome forces of nature. "The Charleston Earthquake" vividly portrayed the effects of the tremor that shook Charleston on August 31, 1886. "New York under the Snow" gave an unforgettable account of city life in the aftermath of the blizzard of 1888. And in 1889 Martí wrote of one of the worst disasters of the decade in his article "Johnstown," about the furious floodwaters that swept through a peaceful Pennsylvania valley.

Along with the fanfare of major events, Martí found time to record quiet moments and everyday scenes. He helped his readers to experience the changing seasons in New York, to envision the different sections of the city, and to feel the pulse of public transportation. He described summertime crowds at Coney Island and offered a charming vignette about two golden orioles spinning a nest in Central Park.

Martí never traveled west of the Alleghenies, but he knew that depictions of the West must be part of his writing. He told of the West's men of legend like Jesse James and Buffalo Bill. And when Buffalo Bill's Wild West Show came to New York, Martí gave his readers a front-row seat. Mexican riders, an Indian medicine man, scenes of everyday Indian activity, cowboy adventures, and the pony express all came to life in his pages. He described the Oklahoma land rush and recorded the addition of new states to the Union—Washington, Montana, North Dakota, and South Dakota.

Finally, Martí dissected U.S. policy toward Latin America, a policy that increasingly injected the colossus into neighbors' affairs. He deplored the desire of U.S. leaders to annex Cuba, decried their covetous gaze toward Haiti and the Dominican Republic, and noted American plans for a canal through Central America. Martí was concerned about United States interest in acquiring more of Mexico, and as a corollary he mentioned American expansion-mindedness in the Pacific.

Conclusions

The decade and a half that Martí spent in the United States was a critical period in his life in every respect. During these years he developed and refined his sociopolitical thought, resolved key issues of his personal life including the failure of his marriage, wrote many of his most important literary works, undertook his major translations, honed his precepts of literary criticism, inspired compatriots to share his vision of *patria,* and established himself as a principal voice for Nuestra América.

All of these factors form the framework for his portrayal of North American life. In turn, this portrait became an important source of information for Spanish Americans seeking to understand the United States, and it made Martí a transnational figure who continues to link the Americas.

Martí and American Authors

Martí's commentary on U.S. literature began even before he arrived in the United States. In 1874, en route from England to Mexico, a stop in New York afforded him an early impression of North America. Among Martí's travel notes is a chronicle that appears to refer to this journey and thus to offer initial observations about American literary life.[1] In these impressions, Martí lamented the immense North American nation's neglect of the arts, stating that the United States had been denied the enlightenment to appreciate "the rhythm of poetry, the echo of music, and the sublime ecstasy that a work of art produces in the soul" (19:17). Such pessimism about American cultural life did not persist, however, once Martí began living in the United States and writing articles for the Latin American press. In Martí's November 1881 column for *La Opinión Nacional*, the change of tone is evident: "North Americans do not excel at drama. They do, however, excel in lyric poetry, which they write with real power, grace, sensitivity, and originality. Those who disdain their talents do not know them. A great variety of motifs and a frankness of tone characterize their poetry. They blend the profound with the delicate, the joyous with the sad, and thus achieve in their verses the true color and look of life" (23:81).

Martí regarded American literature as essential for seeing the United States in proper perspective. In a December 1882 letter he informed the director of *La Nación* that his correspondence for the Buenos Aires paper would provide contrast: "picturesque scenes will balance serious topics and literature will brighten the reporting on politics" (9:17). Martí continued by saying that although Emerson and Longfellow had just died, and Whittier and Holmes were close to the grave, authors such as Henry James and Walt Whitman remained to be studied (9:18). In another instance, Martí emphasized the contrast between the brutality of a boxing match and the good taste of those "who maintain the nation's honor, vote for honest men like Cleveland, influence collegial and sacred matters, and gather to hear Mark Twain and George Cable" (10:134).

Martí's belief in the importance of a nation's literature is clearly indicated in his essay on Walt Whitman: "Who is the fool who maintains that poetry is not indispensable to a people? There are those so shortsighted that they mistake the rind for the fruit. . . . Poetry, whether it unite or divide the soul, comfort or afflict it, uplift or cast it down, whether it give men faith or hope or take them away, is more necessary to a people than industry itself, for while this gives men the means of subsistence, poetry gives men the desire and strength to live" (13:135).[2]

Martí insisted that one could not understand the United States without understanding her men and women of letters. This belief caused Martí to sharply criticize the superficial treatment given to American literature by French author Paul Blouet. Blouet, under the pen name Max O'Rell, had written about the United States in the book *Jonathan and His Continent*. Martí reviewed the book for *El Partido Liberal* and decried the Frenchman's frivolous handling of literature—just a listing of names without comment or analysis. Martí continued by outlining Blouet's omissions: "By listing Whitman, he thinks he's said it all; without knowing who Thoreau was, he declares that North America has no writers who depict nature; and since he is ignorant of Emerson to the point of omitting the name of America's foremost poet, he assures us that the United States has not yet produced a transcendental genius" (12:163).

Martí's plans for his literary legacy also prove his interest in America's literature. In the "literary testament" Martí wrote shortly before his death, he envisioned his prose works being collected into six principal volumes—with three of them about North America. For the two volumes about "North Americans" Martí wanted included his articles on Emerson, Whitman, and Alcott, and stated that his writing contained ample comment about Longfellow and Lanier (20:478).

American literature, whether described through reference to a specific author or alluded to in a less direct manner, is present throughout Martí's writing. Most of his important studies about and references to U.S. authors appear in the articles Martí wrote about the United States and North American life. Comments and references can also be found, however, in his articles about Europe and Latin America, among his letters and notes, in his magazine for children, *La Edad de Oro*, and in his novel,

Amistad funesta.[3] Further, Martí's translations from U.S. literature form a significant part of his treatment of American letters.

Martí's engagement with American literature can be divided into three general categories: sketches, references, and translations. Six sketches or articles deal at length with individual authors, and the writers described in these literary portraits are among Martí's favorites: Ralph Waldo Emerson, Walt Whitman, Henry Wadsworth Longfellow, John Greenleaf Whittier, Amos Bronson Alcott, and Louisa May Alcott. Martí published his essays about Emerson and Longfellow in *La Opinión Nacional* in 1882, and the essay about Whitman in both *La Nación* and *El Partido Liberal* in 1887. The articles about Whittier and the Alcotts appear only in Martí's notes and were apparently not published in his lifetime.

Much of Martí's engagement with U.S. authors was conveyed by brief references in articles that covered various topics. In some cases Martí merely mentioned a name; in other cases he offered a page or two of comment. These discussions of writers and their works within the context of other subjects may make them seem less important, but such references introduced Spanish American readers to a host of major and minor authors and presented U.S. literature as an integral part of the fabric of national life.

Martí's association of a number of authors chiefly with a single event—the copyright benefit held in New York in November of 1887—was a timely and appropriate connection with U.S. literature. Concern over the absence of international copyright protection was a major issue for American authors in the 1880s. Both legal and ethical considerations formed part of the debate and the topic enjoyed wide press coverage. The *Century's* February 1888 issue, for example, issued a call for reform and reported on remarks given by James Russell Lowell: "Mr. Lowell, in presiding over the very successful Author's Readings in New York last November, added to the number of his admirable sayings in favor of international copyright."[4] The magazine quoted from arguments Lowell had used in his plea to a committee of Congress and noted part of his Chickering Hall address: "To steal a book I have bought is theft; to steal a book I have made—what is that?"[5] Martí made note of Lowell's prominent role at the authors' reading at Chickering Hall and named writers of both romanticism and realism in connection with the event.

Helen Hunt Jackson, author of *Ramona*. Courtesy of the Library of Congress, Prints and Photographs Division (LC-USZ62-122761).

Martí was a skillful translator who rendered literary pieces from both French and English into Spanish. While still a boy in Cuba, well before he published his translation of Victor Hugo's *Mes Fils*, he had tried his hand at translating portions of *Hamlet* and of Byron's *Cain, a Mystery*. In the 1880s he translated Thomas Moore's *Lalla Rookh*, though this translation was apparently lost (20:477). In New York, Martí also used his translating talents to earn a living, doing contract work for Appleton and Company. This work included translating Hugh Conway's popular novel *Called Back*—a work Martí titled *Misterio* in translation.

The question of what constitutes translation—and of how translation, paraphrasing, and adaptation may overlap—is germane to Martí's work, since examples of each can be found in his writing on American authors. The parameters of translation are variable and may differ according to specific theories and methods.[6] In this text, translation is defined broadly. Examples of paraphrasing and literary adaptation are identified as such when there can be little doubt as to their categorization.

Martí's interest in translation provided a means through which American writing entered his own opus. In his essays about American authors and in briefer references, Martí conveyed many descriptive passages, thoughts, and even fragments from U.S. writers. In the realm of poetry, Martí translated from Helen Hunt Jackson, Emerson, Whitman, Longfellow, Poe, Whittier, and John Howard Payne. He translated lines from Emerson's essays, portions of Louisa May Alcott's *Hospital Sketches*, a toast to literature given by Lowell, and lines from Thoreau, Charles Dudley Warner, and George Willliam Curtis. In 1888 the Cuban writer published, on his own account and out of deep personal interest, his translation of the novel *Ramona*.

Helen Hunt Jackson's *Ramona* occupies a distinctive place in Martí's literary links to the United States. This work attracted Martí's attention because of the author's role as a champion of the American Indian and because of the novel's depiction of Anglo versus Spanish treatment of the Indians in California. Martí endorsed Jackson's sympathies and saw her work as a positive expression of American writing. At the same time, he conceived of his translation as a political warning to Mexico about U.S. interests—a book that revealed American lack of regard for indigenous people and the nation's expansionist eye toward the borderlands.

Martí's long look at American literature, which began before his arrival in New York and continued throughout the U.S. years, was informed by text—the literary works themselves—and by context, or the ambience in which publications came to press. Martí's selections were sound, his assessments judicious, and his scope comprehensive. He devoted major attention to three giants of the nineteenth-century American literary scene—Emerson, Whitman, and Longfellow—and made allusion to thirty-seven other authors.

This study does not cover writers known primarily for work outside of literature, such as historian George Bancroft. Also excluded are nineteenth-century authors whose names no longer resonate as significant, Amelie Rives for example, and English-born authors like Hugh Conway. Clarence Stedman, an essayist, poet, and editor, was cited twice in Martí's writing as a "good critic" and was quoted very briefly in the Emerson essay, but essentially Martí regarded him as a critic rather than as a literary figure.

Let us therefore, following Martí's lead, begin at the top of the class with Emerson.

4

Martí and Emerson

Kindred Souls

Martí never met Emerson and in all likelihood knew nothing of the author or his works before coming to the United States. Yet once begun, Martí's engagement with Emerson was intense, and this American author's impact is the single most significant example of the way in which literature and literary figures imparted a positive reading of the United States for Martí.

Martí's interest in Emerson began when the expatriate Cuban had taken up residence in the United States and begun to feel the literary pulse of the nation. Occasional references appeared in Martí's writing in 1881, but not until May 1882 did Martí's passion for his "kindred soul" burst forth in almost unparalleled exuberance. Following Emerson's death in Concord, Massachusetts, on April 27, 1882, news, tributes, and commentaries filled the pages of the American press and brought the transcendentalist fully to Martí's attention. With trembling hand Martí took up his pen to portray Emerson for readers of *La Opinión Nacional*, charting a voyage of autodiscovery in the process. The essay on Emerson, published in the Caracas newspaper on May 19, radiates apprehension and excitement and is the starting point for any treatment of the ties between Martí and Emerson.

Martí's Essay about Emerson

Martí's essay on Emerson is an impressive literary portrait, a recapitulation of newspaper accounts, a meeting of the minds, and a major enterprise in translation. After it appeared in *La Opinión Nacional*, its circulation in Spanish-speaking countries helped to make Emerson more widely known in Spanish America. And among North Americans, through its translation into English, it has become one of the better known of Martí's articles about the United States. Three excellent translations of the essay are available in English: a version by Juan de Onís imparts the flavor and resonance of the original; one by Luis Baralt is more studied and literal; a recent rendering by Esther Allen is also highly successful.[1]

Martí's palpable excitement in approaching Emerson set the tone for the entire essay. Martí scholar Ivan Schulman has convincingly connected the tenor and pitch of the *obra martiana* to the author's emotional state and shown how much of Martí's best writing built upon feelings of pleasure. Martí's work took on fervent qualities in accord with his admiration for the subject, and nowhere is this more true than with Emerson. Martí's choice of colors and symbols was developed consistently, and he selected his loftiest symbols and chromatic schemes in writing of Emerson.[2] Unfurling with a flourish a banner of praise, Martí likened Emerson to a mountain, symbol of a superior being; represented him through such words as "eagle" and "pine," symbols of energy and greatness; associated his character with "star," the Martí symbol for ideal human qualities and tendencies; represented the free flight of Emerson's inspiration as "butterfly of fire"; and symbolized the poet's verses as "wings of gold." The color white, a positive color for Martí, added to the exemplary nature of the description.[3]

Martí's Emerson was superior, noble, and elevated, his death victorious, his hearse a triumphal chariot with palms strewn below and swords raised on high. And Martí described the author of *Nature* on nature's terms: a clifflike brow, aquiline nose, pine-sturdy bearing. He was a mountain, a monument, a supreme being—one of a class of emperors, with "priestly," "angelic," and "Mosaic" qualities. Emerson, according to Martí, was resplendent, starlike, and bathed in light. His house peaked upward with a high roof—an indication of the upward flow of ideas. The Emerson presented in Martí's essay was a monarch, a lion, and a giant in the realm of ideas. Emerson the man embodied purity and virtue. His works were lucid, his pages radiant. For Martí, reading Emerson filled the mind with light and kindled the soul.

The spiritual affinity Martí developed for Emerson is the more remarkable in view of the seeming disparity between the two authors. Martí, slightly built, his intense face filled with a bushy mustache, the product of a colonized society, an exile, a man living on the margins eco-

Ralph Waldo Emerson, Martí's kindred soul. Courtesy of the Library of Congress, Prints and Photographs Division (LC-USZ62-116399).

nomically and emotionally, a husband bedeviled by an unhappy marriage, and a patriot consumed by the politics of his fatherland, fell heroically at age forty-two on the battlefield. Emerson, tall, clean-shaven, of angular features, a citizen of a colossus poised to colonize, a son of New England, and a successful writer with a tranquil family life, died peacefully at age seventy-nine at his comfortable Massachusetts home.

Notwithstanding the disparities of background and bearing, Martí's identification with Emerson in his 1882 essay is so complete that at times it is difficult to determine what refers to Emerson and what to Martí. The Cuban writer took sentences from the book *Nature* and then elaborated and interpreted them in his own framework.[4] When Martí commented on Emerson's joy as a father he seemed to be remembering his own son's birth. Testimony to the affinity between writer and subject is the fact that Martí's tribute was, in matters of style, not unlike Emerson's own work: Emerson's essays used repetition, illustration, examples, and a scattering of eminently quotable lines, and Martí's essay about him had the same characteristics.

The essay is a tapestry of ideas rather than a progression of thoughts. Martí began by expressing humility in writing of a great figure, and hailed Emerson as victorious over death—a warrior surrounded by the signs of triumph, the sword and the palm. In the first part of the essay Martí wrote of Emerson's fame, background, home, general pattern of thinking, and style of writing. Then he discussed the transcendentalist's ideas on nature, mentioned several of his works, and expounded on his "philosophy." In the last part of the essay Martí quoted directly a number of Emerson's thoughts about God and nature, man and nature, and science and the soul. At various points in the essay he noted Emerson's sources. He also alluded to Emerson's attitude toward death. Martí closed the literary tribute in a manner that made Emerson's triumph complete: "Marvelous old man, at your feet I place my sheaf of green palms and my silver sword" (13:30).

The essay on Emerson, besides revealing the Cuban writer's respect for his subject, provided basic information for Latin American readers. Martí mentioned the American writer's slim, tall frame and lean and angular face, and the fact that Emerson had been slight and timid as a boy. He described Emerson's home in Concord—a city Martí considered sacred—as a shrine to freedom, and related how Emerson personally received visitors to the home and served them sherry at his mahogany table. Martí wrote that Emerson was educated for the clergy but had given up a religious calling. Emerson read many books but had not fallen into the trap of imitation; instead he added a new voice. Martí called Emerson a writer of renown and underscored the importance of knowing about a man "whom all the world knows" (13:18).

To confirm Emerson's significance, Martí offered quotations from Carlyle, Whitman, Stedman, and Alcott. He noted Emerson's sources: Montaigne, Swedenborg, Plotinus, Plato, and the sacred books of the Hindus. Martí's article referenced *Nature* and *English Traits*, made allusions to *Representative Men* and to Emerson's essays, and expressed a number of Emerson's basic concepts.

Sometimes Martí quoted directly from Emerson, putting the quote into Spanish for his readers; at other times he paraphrased Emerson's thoughts; in still other instances he took ideas from Emerson and interpreted them in his own way. The similarities in thinking and style between Martí and Emerson, and the rhapsodic nature of the essay, make it difficult to establish exactly what material in Martí's essay originated with Emerson. Nonetheless it is possible to identify many lines either as direct quotes, as paraphrases of Emerson's writing, or as apparently inspired by Emerson—and to see that, through this medley of references, Martí rendered a comprehensive representation of Emerson's work.

Most of the ideas conveyed in the essay were from *Nature*, which contained much of Emerson's basic philosophy. Martí described Emerson as living "face to face with nature," and as one to whom nature revealed herself (13:18). He wrote that Emerson saw what he saw, felt what he felt, and related it without pretense. He proclaimed that those who failed to understand Emerson were lesser minds incapable of comprehending the thinking of a great mind (13:19). Martí paraphrased lines from the first part of *Nature:* "El veía detrás de sí al Espíritu creador que a través de él hablaba a la naturaleza. El se veía como pupila transparente que lo veía todo, lo reflejaba todo, y sólo era pupila" (13:19).[5] According to Martí, Emerson preferred nature's teachings to man's and felt that nature could teach more than a book or a university. Following this line of thinking, Martí said in an apparent reference to part 5 of *Nature:* "una hacienda es un evangelio."[6] Emerson's awe before the beauty of nature was communicated in another paraphrase: "Se siente más poderoso que monarca asirio o rey de Persia, cuando asiste a una puesta de sol, o a un alba riente" (13:22).[7]

Martí wrote that Emerson wanted to delve into the mystery of life and to discover the laws of the universe, and that he enjoyed the peace of mind of a man who had sought the Creator and found Him (13:23). Martí proclaimed the American author a herald of new ideas, called *Nature* his best book, and insisted that Emerson found only analogies in nature and saw no contradictions in the universal creation (13:23). The Cuban writer expounded on Emerson's idea that "nature always wears the colors of the spirit" (13:23).[8]

Martí credited Emerson with seeing nature as a teacher, with understanding the universality of creation, and with believing in a central unity in events, thoughts, and actions (13:24). He quoted Emerson on the importance of virtue: "la virtud es la llave de oro que abre las puertas de la Eternidad" (13:24).[9] He also may have been thinking of a passage in *Nature* when he wrote: "la vida no es más que una estación en la naturaleza" (13:24).[10] Martí noted in part 8 of *Nature* the belief that the soul is superior to science in discovering universal truths, that science confirms the experience of the soul, and that science is not false, just slow (13:25).[11] Martí included Emerson's example—according to Martí a sort of foreshadowing of the evolutionary theory—that the flipper of the saurus is similar to the human hand (13:25).[12]

The Cuban author expressed Emerson's concept that satisfaction of the desire for perfect beauty is the object of life and described beauty in its broader sense as moral beauty (virtue), beauty of the intellect (judgment), and pure beauty, which gives delight in and of itself (13:25).[13] Martí noted Emerson's statement that "El arte no es más que la naturaleza creada por el hombre" (13:25).[14] He also conveyed Emerson's idea that nature perfects man's judgment by showing him her differences, enlivens his spirit of imitation by displaying her marvels, and strengthens his character by presenting exigencies and vicissitudes (13:25).[15] Martí repeated Emerson's suggestion that the stars are messengers of beauty—"Los astros son mensajeros de hermosuras y de lo sublime perpetuo" (13:25)[16]—and that the forest renews man: "El bosque vuelve al hombre a la razón y a la fe, y es juventud perpetua" (13:25).[17]

Martí then noted the American author's idea of nature displaying the characteristics of the human spirit, and he paraphrased Emerson on the subject of nature's unity in variety: "El Universo con ser múltiple es uno: la música puede imitar el movimiento y los colores de la serpiente. La locomotora es la creación del hombre, potente y colosal como los elefantes. Sólo el grado de calor hace diversas el agua que corre por el cauce del río y las piedras que el río baña" (13:26).[18] Martí también tomó Emerson's idea that each quality of man was represented in nature— "Cada cualidad del hombre está representada en un animal de la naturaleza" (13:26)[19]—and mentioned the perspective expressed in part 6 of *Nature*: "El Hombre, frente a la naturaleza que cambia y pasa, siente en sí algo estable" (13:26).[20] Martí credited Emerson with profound and original thinking and said the transcendentalist believed that both reason and understanding were needed to comprehend the mystery of life (13:29).[21] Martí paraphrased Emerson's concept: "es que el eje de la visión del hombre no coincide con el eje de la naturaleza" (13:29).[22] And he expressed Emerson's thought that moral and physical truths are contained in one another: "son como los círculos de una circumferencia, que se comprenden todos los unos a los otros, y entran y salen libremente sin que ninguno esté por encima de otro" (13:29).[23]

Martí offered other thoughts from *Nature*. He gave as direct quotations: "Para un hombre que sufre, el calor de su propia chimenea tiene tristeza" (13:30)[24]; "No estamos hechos como buques, para ser sacudidos, sino como edificios para estar en firme" (13:30)[25]; "Leónidas consumió un día en morir" (13:30)[26]; and "Estériles como un solo sexo son los hechos de la historia natural, tomados por sí mismos" (13:30).[27]

In addition to the many references to *Nature*, Martí's essay made allusions to other works by Emerson and included an overview of his poetry. In the early part of the essay Martí called Emerson's verses "flights of angels" (13:18) and said Emerson's poetry and prose were echoes of each other (13:19). His most telling comment on Emerson's poetry came at the end of the article: "His is a poetry of patriarchs, primitive men, cyclops. Some of his poems are like an oak grove in bloom. His poetry is the only one that consecrates the greatest struggle on earth. And other poems of his are like brooks of precious stones: or patches of clouds, or a bolt of lightning" (13:30).[28]

Martí continued in a similar vein, but this paragraph—a sequence of impressions—gives no definitive clue as to which Emerson poems he may have read or intended to reference. One line that invites conjecture is "Suyos son los únicos versos poémicos que consagran la lucha magna de esta tierra" (13:30), which Luis Baralt translated as "He wrote the only truly poetic verse on this country's great struggle."[29] Baralt's translation is probably closer to Martí's intent than the above-quoted rendering by Juan de Onís—"His poetry is the only one that consecrates the greatest struggle on earth"—but, as Baralt acknowledges, the meaning is open to interpretation.[30]

Perhaps Martí was referring to America's struggle for independence and perhaps specifically to the poem "Concord Hymn." This is possible, since Martí wrote frequently and with admiration of the American struggle for independence and sought independence for his own country. Or the line may have referred to America's struggle over the slavery question and to "Boston Hymn." A critic for the *North American Review* intimated in 1880 that this Emerson poem reflected a mighty struggle.[31] Still another possibility is that Martí was referring to the labor-capital conflicts of North America's Gilded Age. Martí called these opposing forces the "worms" and the "eagles," and the struggle in the United States between forces of corruption and voices of reform figured repeatedly in his writing.[32]

Martí wrote about Emerson's prose, calling *Representative Men* a marvelous book, a summary of human experience (13:28), and describing England, home of Emerson's puritan fathers, as a source for the powerful work *English Traits* (13:28). According to Martí, the American philosopher and poet wrote "magical essays" in which he grouped and studied the facts of life (13:28). Martí also mentioned Emerson's laws of life, and the last two lines of the poem "Wealth," which precedes the essay of the same title. He said that all of Emerson's laws revolved around the truth that "toda la naturaleza tiembla ante la conciencia de un niño" (13:28).[33] Martí listed several chapters of *The Conduct of Life*, without naming the work itself, and declared that Emerson had thoroughly analyzed each topic. In Martí's words, "El culto, el destino, el poder, la riqueza, las ilusiones, la grandeza, fueron por él como por mano de químico, descompuestos y analizados" (13:28).[34] Of Emerson's essays, Martí wrote that they were like codes, exuded wisdom, and displayed the grand monotony of a range of mountains (13:29). Martí also hailed Emerson's breadth of vision and singular good sense (13:29).

Among the quoted Emerson works other than *Nature* were "The Over-Soul," "Self-Reliance," and "Montaigne; or, the Skeptic." Emerson maintained that "dentro del hombre está el alma del conjunto, la del sabio silencio, la hermosura universal, a la que toda parte y partícula está igualmente relacionada: el Uno Eterno" (13:24).[35] From "Self-Reliance" Martí quoted the familiar maxim "Ser grande es no ser entendido" (13:30),[36] and from the essay on Montaigne in *Representative Men* he selected the sentence "Cortad estas palabras, y sangrarán" (13:30).[37]

Finally, Martí touched briefly on the American author's style and method. He saw Emerson as an observer, not a mediator, and declared that everything he wrote was a maxim (13:22). Martí appeared to contemplate with pleasure the joy of thinking experienced by a lofty mind such as Emerson's and described the Emersonian style as sculpted and pure, with all unnecessary verbiage clipped away (13:22). For Martí, Emerson was a writer who avoided wasting time, moved in the realm of ideas, and announced rather than explained; when he described the enslavement of men, his words poured forth with the power of biblical wrath (13:22).

Martí also proposed that Emerson had something of Calderón, of Plato, of Pindar, and of Franklin (13:29). He emphasized the strength and lack of pretense in Emerson's style, explaining that Emerson was like a firm tree with a sturdy trunk rather than a leafy, showy plant (13:29).

Martí observed in Emerson a custom similar to his own—collecting and jotting down ideas in notebooks (13:29). And Martí's own essay on Emerson reflected Emerson's tendency to crowd ideas together in an effort to include all and forget nothing. Martí's tribute to Emerson leaped from idea to idea, attempting to get everything said. Such an approach was vintage Martí as well as a faithful reflection of Emerson.

References in Articles and Notes

The essay written in May of 1882 is Martí's most important and lengthy comment on Emerson. However, another segment nearly four pages long and titled "Emerson" also offers significant information about the American author. This passage, part of Martí's notes and reviews, is undated and apparently was never published. Nonetheless, it gives an idea of what Martí considered most important about Emerson. Most of the passage is typewritten, but some lines are written by hand and a few words are illegible. Much of it is fragmentary and notelike, and in some instances transitions are not clear.

The first five paragraphs read more smoothly than the rest and, except for the fourth paragraph, manifest a coherence not evident as the passage goes on. Martí may have worked on the first part previously: among his notes and fragments, believed to have been written between 1885 and 1895, are paragraphs that look like rough drafts for the first part of the "notebook" segment on Emerson (22:156–57).

The first three paragraphs all incorporate the concept that Emerson moved in a realm of major intellectual inquiry. Ideas came to him in quantity and with such suddenness and disorder that he was able to incorporate only the most significant, leaving lesser ideas behind. According to Martí, Emerson's restriction to the current of principal ideas made his writing seem confusing to simple men. For Martí, Emerson was an eagle, who soared above those not ready for such majesty (19:353–54).

In this extensive notebook comment on the American writer, several points evident in the published essay are present. Martí mentioned the purity of Emerson's life and works, and praised his comprehension of nature and maturity of experience. Martí viewed Emerson as a man who thought for himself, and he spent the whole first page of this entry explaining how the author gathered and organized ideas. Martí emphasized that ideas presented themselves to Emerson piecemeal, not in neat bouquets of flowers. At one point the Cuban writer seemed almost envious of Emerson's independence in his work—which meant that thoughts could be put down when they were ready, not squeezed out before their time. Yet for the most part, in writing about the way ideas come to a writer, Martí could have been referring to himself as well as to Emerson.

The most extensive comment on Emerson, excluding the essay and the notebook material, was a brief piece for the "Sección Constante" of May 23, 1882. This comment, which closely followed the appearance of the essay on Emerson in *La Opinión Nacional,* served some of the same functions. It stressed Emerson's importance, named several of his works, and gave information about his writing. Appearing only four days after the essay, and in the same newspaper, it may have served chiefly as a reinforcement. Yet there are notable differences between the essay and the "Sección Constante" reference, and each contributed in its own way to acquainting Caracas readers with Emerson.

In the column Martí's comment was, of necessity, brief, and the writing more ordered and factual. Martí dealt first with Emerson the man and his image, then with Emerson's prose works, and finally with his poetry. He highlighted Emerson's importance, saying that the American writer was highly esteemed, widely recognized as one of the greatest American poets, and called a modern Plato because of his profound insight, his love of the perfect, and his veneration of beauty.

On Emerson's prose works, the Cuban writer began by mentioning several ideas from *Nature:* that mind is superior to matter; that man, who has limits, will go unto a Creator who is limitless; that nature's purpose is to serve and to educate man; and that the object of life is to prepare, through the exercise of virtue, for a happy passing. Martí mentioned *Representative Men,* which he said could also be called "Mystic Men," and he listed the various types Emerson included: Montaigne the skeptic, Plato the philosopher, Swedenborg the mystic, Shakespeare the poet, Goethe the writer, and Napoleon the man of the world. Martí praised the power of concentration revealed in *Representative Men,* calling it an amazing book where each sentence was a profound statement in and of itself. Martí noted *English Traits* as a work that analyzed and described

England. He reported that Emerson's *Essays* brought together the essence of the author's reading and touched on virtually every subject of importance to mankind. Then Martí gave the titles of some of Emerson's essay collections: *The Conduct of Life, Society and Solitude,* and *Letters and Social Aims.*

Martí also wrote about Emerson's verses, saying that the poetic résumés that he placed at the head of his essays were remarkable. Martí called "Threnody" an "august elegy" and "perhaps the most sober, great, and heartfelt expression of fatherly grief to be found in any language" (23:305–6). He also considered "May-Day" a superior work, saying that not even among Greek classics or the English pastoral poems was there a descriptive poem to surpass it. "Its descriptive passages," he wrote, "are like the translation which the American poet Bryant made of the *Iliad.* But Emerson's rhythm is more spirited and uplifting than Bryant's" (23:306).

In the "Sección Constante" piece on Emerson, Martí listed more titles and gave more attention to specific poems than he had in the essay; he said comparatively less about Emerson's prose works and *Nature.* Martí's comment that Emerson had declared mind superior to matter in the book *Nature* is subject to contention. Martí may have felt the concept settled to his satisfaction, but critics point to the mind-matter question as one of *Nature's* unresolved problems.[38] Martí's assessment of Emerson's poetry is arguably more discerning.

In writing for Spanish American newspapers, Martí made brief comments about Emerson's style. In an 1890 article for *El Partido Liberal,* Martí wrote that American poetry offered "the mystery of Poe, the prophetic ode of Emerson, and the revolutionary rhythm of Walt Whitman" (5:190). In one case he noted "that profound language of Emerson" (13:41), and in an 1883 article for *La América* he praised Emerson's "resplendent verses" (13:420).

The preeminence of the Northeast in American literature provided another context for allusions to the Concord poet. In an 1884 article for *La América,* Martí wrote that Massachusetts was home to "Emerson, a more pleasing Dante, who lived above the earth more than on it . . . and who wrote a human Bible" (8:427). In an 1883 reference in *La Nación,* Martí noted Emerson as being from Boston (9:338). Other times he mentioned Boston as "the city of Emerson" (11:265) or as the place "in whose surrounding areas Emerson thought" (11:25).

Martí mentioned Emerson frequently in connection with other U.S. authors. When he wrote of Longfellow's death, he listed writers present at the interment and said that among those honoring Longfellow's memory was Emerson, "in whose craggy face was painted the solemn and majestic composure of one feeling the imminent approach of his own eternal rest" (13:230–31). In his essay on Whitman, Martí said: "Emerson, whose works purify and exalt, threw an arm around his [Whitman's] shoulder and called him a friend" (13:132). In writing on Amos Bronson Alcott, Martí noted Emerson's support for his friend's decision against using corporal punishment on schoolchildren: "Your system is just, said Emerson, who was never afraid to defend the cause of forsaken reason" (13:189). In the same article, Alcott was called "a companion of the august Emerson" (13:187). In his article on Louisa May Alcott, Martí noted that she grew up in a country setting near Thoreau and Hawthorne and "that white eagle named Emerson" (13:193). A piece on Whittier referred to Emerson as one of the writers of the "Homeric era of American letters" (13:403).

In Martí's notes, as well, Emerson was often grouped with American writers. Several passages in Martí's notes indicate that he envisioned a book that would include as subjects Emerson, Motley, Longfellow, and Whitman (22:116). And when Martí translated Helen Hunt Jackson's *Ramona*, the introduction spoke of the "good sense" of Jackson's friend Emerson (24:204).

While Martí frequently linked Emerson with the Northeast or authors from New England, Emerson's name appeared in a variety of accounts about U.S. life. Martí's 1888 article on Courtlandt Palmer mentioned the socialist millionaire's interest in authors like Emerson and Holmes (13:353). The 1889 centennial of Washington's oath of office occasioned another mention. Martí described the patriotic spirit surrounding the event and wrote that in the schools children were being taught verses by Emerson, Lowell, and Whittier—verses that celebrated "'el cañonazo que dio la vuelta al mundo,'[39] 'el aire que respiraron Dekalb y Sumter,'[40] 'el suelo que nos dio este hombre imperial'" (13:503).[41] Martí also touched on Emerson in writing about current books. In an 1883 article for *La Nación*, Martí mentioned a work in which "Carlyle and Emerson speak alternately in letters" (9:413)—a reference, no doubt, to Charles Eliot Norton's 1883 edition of *The Correspondence of Emerson and Carlyle*. He continued by describing Emerson's high forehead and broad temples. Within this noble frame, said Martí, "an eternal light shone" (9:413). Emerson and Carlyle were contrasted—Carlyle as the coldly cerebral writer, Emerson as the man of human warmth (9:413).

In a review of Enrique José Varona's *Seis conferencias* published in *El Economista Americano* in 1888, Martí studied a Cuban compatriot's treatment of Emerson and observed that Varona had described the unapparent similarities between the idealistic Emerson and his commercially oriented nation (5:119). Martí further commented on Varona's study of the American author: "Emerson seems less radiant, almost as if revealed through his verses on the ransomed sphinx; yet he is there with his blue eyes and imperial mien, his lofty pace and his astral philosophy. And he is there with the imposing resolution of his pure spirit—a witness to the universal and to the spiritual and harmonic marvel of nature. This is the Emerson who, ten years before Darwin, saw the worm in its struggle to become like man 'mounting through all the spires of form'" (5:120).

Martí particularly liked Emerson's idea that the poet might discover truth before the scientist did. In correspondence for *El Partido Liberal* Martí suggested that the universe presented a challenge for both science and literature and added: "Emerson the observer said the same thing as Edison the mechanic: the latter working with details and the former looking at the total picture" (11:164). In another reference, this one for *La América* in 1883, Martí mentioned Emerson's contribution to Tyndall's thinking as an example of the insights about nature that a poet might provide (23:17).

Martí was beguiled by the idea that Emerson had anticipated the theory of evolution in two lines that prefaced the second edition of *Nature:* "And, striving to be man, the worm / Mounts through all the spires of form" (21:391). This idea appeared repeatedly in Martí's writing and notes. One of the lengthiest comments was published in *La Nación* in 1890 when Martí wrote about Chautauqua. He described a man rising and saying: "In my town we've always said that poets see the truth before anyone else, and this conversation proves it because men are no more than grown worms, which is what Emerson said, before Darwin, when he said that in his struggle to be man the worm rises from form to form" (12:435). In the same article Martí mentioned another man reciting Emerson's verses (12:435).

Emerson's universality of spirit won enthusiastic approval from Martí. In an 1887 article for *El Partido Liberal* Martí described Charles

Dudley Warner's account of a trip to Mexico and used these comments to contrast Warner's narrow-mindedness with Emerson's universality. Warner was unable to sympathize with Mexico, an attitude Martí attributed to the writer's desire to confine himself to those of his own race and style, and to judge everything by that standard. Martí saw Emerson, on the other hand, as a man who appreciated the essence of the human spirit evident in all people. For Martí, Emerson was an emperor and Warner an ensign; Emerson's embrace of humanity was broad and Warner's outlook on mankind was narrow (7:54–55). Later in the year this same example was repeated in an article for *La Nación* (7:331).

Emerson had an important role in Martí's magazine for children, *La Edad de Oro*. Martí envisioned the magazine as a vehicle for presenting ennobling examples of literature and as a way of highlighting significant concepts and figures of renown. He noted Emerson's declaration that no literary work could match the power of a well-lived life—especially the story of a brave man who has done his duty (18:391). He also translated Emerson's poem "Fable" for *La Edad de Oro*.

While most of what Martí wrote on Emerson appeared in print, significant material can be found in Martí's notes. Many of these notebook references are brief and/or fragmentary: "From Emerson—celestial sentences" (21:39), or "The profound goodness of Emerson's face" (22:141). A brief note in English began: "Mr. Emerson's essays are gathered from his journals" (21:379). Martí believed that good literature did not always sell well and that good books had often been refused by printers. He noted that Emerson's *Nature* sold only five hundred copies in twelve years (21:396), and questioned how well Carlyle's *Sartor Resartus* would have done without Emerson's help (21:430).

Direct quotations from Emerson also appear in Martí's notes, for example: "The distinction and end of a soundly constituted man is his labor" (21:391), from "The Fortune of the Republic,"[42] and "—The greatest spirit only attaining to humility" (21:391), from "American Civilization."[43] Another quotation, given in English and cited more than once in Martí's notes, was: "The world is mind precipitated" (21:408), from the essay "Nature" in *Emerson's Essays: Second Series*.[44] Martí also noted a comment about critics from Emerson's "Poetry and Imagination": "The critic destroys: the poet says nothing but what helps somebody" (21:421).[45]

Still another revelation in Martí's notebooks is the intensity of his feeling for the American author. Among the entries is this passage: "I have journeyed through much of life and partaken of its various pleasures, but the greatest pleasure, the only absolutely pure pleasure that I have experienced up to this point, was the one I felt that afternoon, when I looked out from my room to the prostrate city and envisioned the future, thinking about Emerson" (22:323). In another instance Martí placed the afternoon of Emerson first among the supreme moments in his life, "those few moments one remembers as summits of one's life; the hours that count" (18:288). By this term, Martí apparently meant those moments when a person could be lost in reverie with nature. Clearly these moments provided both encouragement and consolation (21:370).

Martí's notes and comments confirm his continuing interest in Emerson. He found in the transcendentalist an inspiration for his own life, and he saw Emerson's spirit as a contrast to the selfish interests at work in the United States (10:63). Martí's numerous references to Emerson show that he valued Emerson's insights personally as well as professionally and that he wrote of Emerson for personal satisfaction as well as for publication.

Translations

Martí did not comment extensively on Emerson's poetry, but it obviously held interest for him, since he undertook the translation of at least five poems. Knowledge of several of these is relatively recent; as late as 1950 it was believed that Martí had translated only one Emerson poem, the one found in *La Edad de Oro*.[46] Since then, more of Martí's writing has been discovered. Now the verse translations by Martí are included in his *Obras Completas*.

The only Emerson translation published during Martí's lifetime was "Fable," which Martí titled "Cada uno a su oficio" (To Each His Own) and included in *La Edad de Oro*. In this poem, the only Emerson verses Martí rendered in finished form, a humble squirrel explains to a mighty mountain that each of them—one large and magnificent, the other small and agile—has a purpose and place in the larger scheme of things and that each is worthy in his own way. Such a line of thinking is vintage Martí and represented the kind of thinking he wished to instill in his young readers. Furthermore, the Emerson poem is thematically linked to the other major poems of *La Edad de Oro*, "Los dos príncipes" (a version of Helen Hunt Jackson's "The Prince Is Dead") and "Los zapaticos de rosa" (a Martí classic in which a rich child shares her slippers with a poor child), in a progression of poetry depicting the essential nobility of all of nature's facets. In each of the poems Martí sought to provide examples of generosity of spirit that would unite great and small, noble and plebian, rich and poor.[47]

There are Spanish versions of "The World-Soul," which is listed under the title "Emerson," and "Good-Bye," which Martí titled "Adiós Mundo"; however, neither was put into publishable form. Both poems are in the 1963–73 edition of Martí's *Obras Completas* under the category "Poetry/Translations."

Still two other poems, not listed as translations but included in the material in Martí's notebooks, are "The Test" and "Blight." Both the original and a translation of the first four lines of "The Test" are in notes believed to have been written in 1882 (22:261), and fragments of "Blight" come from notes tentatively dated 1885–95 (22:328). Martí's version of "Blight" was identified as a translation from Emerson in 1973.[48]

For the most part Martí was able to capture the cadence and feeling of each poem, although he did not always achieve a rhyme scheme parallel to that of the original. In "Fable," which in translation had twenty-two lines rather than the original nineteen, Martí very nearly duplicated Emerson's rhyme. The last eight lines of the translation, where the squirrel is speaking, illustrate Martí's success.

> Usted no es tan pequeña
> Como yo, ni a gimnástica me enseña.
> Yo negar no imagino
> Que es para las ardillas buen camino
> Su magnífica falda:
> Difieren los talentos a las veces:
> Ni yo llevo los bosques a la espalda,
> Ni usted puede, señora, cascar nueces. (18:325)[49]

The seven corresponding lines from Emerson are:

> You are not so small as I,
> And not half so spry.
> I'll not deny you make

A very pretty squirrel track;
Talents differ; all is well and wisely put;
If I cannot carry forests on my back,
Neither can you crack a nut.[50]

In "The World-Soul," where Emerson maintained an *a-b-c-b-d-e-f-e* rhyme, Martí's translation achieved only an assonant rhyme, generally *a-b-a-b*, and for "Good-Bye," where most of the stanzas in the original were *a-a-b-b-c-c-d-d*, Martí attempted only partially to follow an assonant *a-a-b-b-c-c-d-d* scheme in translation. The beginning lines from "The Test" had an *a-a-b-b* rhyme that Martí did not preserve in translation. For "Blight," from which fragments were translated, neither Emerson nor Martí developed consistent rhyme. Martí's "unpublished" translations were imperfect especially in regard to rhyme, but they were rough drafts. In the case of a finished product such as "Cada uno a su oficio," Martí was highly successful.

Reflections of Emerson in *Versos sencillos*

Emerson was an author to whom Martí (re)turned repeatedly, like a trusted friend. The seduction of Emerson's ideas, subtle yet perceptible, was such that they permeated Martí's work after 1882. This reflection can be glimpsed in the "autobiographical" poetry written during a stay in the Catskill Mountains, a setting not unlike Emerson's surroundings. One of the first to describe an Emersonian flavor in Martí's *Versos sencillos* was Gonzalo de Quesada y Miranda, who linked lines from the first poem of *Versos sencillos*—"Yo vengo de todas partes, / Y hacia todas partes voy: / Arte soy entre las artes; / En los montes, monte soy"—to Emerson's philosophy and his profound communion with nature.[51] Emerson's "Good-Bye," which Martí translated, and the Cuban poet's poem III from *Versos sencillos* share a common theme—the superiority of nature, with its beauty and inspiration, over the noisy crowd—although the development of the theme and the rhyme scheme of the two poems are quite different. José Ballón, in an impressive study, establishes a connection between Emerson's "A Mountain Grave" and poem XXIII of *Versos sencillos*, showing how Emerson's verses are distilled in Martí's.[52] "A Mountain Grave" is one of Emerson's early poems and describes death as triumph. The body is received by and at rest with nature; the corpse returns to earth; the grave cloths are leaves; and the sun confers decency. Martí's poem parallels these sentiments: "I wish to leave this world / In the most natural way. / So in a bed of leaves / Let them carry me away. / Place me not in darkness / For the traitor's lot I shun. / I am good, and like a good man / I will die facing the sun!"[53] In addition, many stanzas in the poems of *Versos sencillos* reflect general aspects of Emerson's philosophy that were mentioned by Martí in his prose writing about the American transcendentalist.

Similarities between Martí and Emerson

Scholars have highlighted the similarities between Martí and Emerson. Manuel Pedro González, in a book published in 1953, the centenary of Martí's birth, stated: "There is a striking similarity between the two in many respects, notwithstanding the cultural, religious, and individual peculiarities that separate them. . . . Both epitomized and symbolized the finest human values of their respective peoples."[54] Esther Elise Shuler listed vigor, identification with nature, sincerity, and metric flexibility as poetic qualities shared by Emerson and Martí and declared that they were alike in their vision of nature. For Shuler both authors embraced a concept of analogies that envisioned all things in nature bearing a relation to one another.[55] Félix Lizaso attributed the Emerson-Martí similarities to their like positions about life and man and to their shared concerns in the realm of spiritual values, and postulated that duty, virtue, generosity, and tenderness were essential to both writers.[56] José Ballón's *Autonomía cultural americana: Emerson y Martí* gives a full discussion of this topic and documents the message of American cultural autonomy preached and practiced by both Emerson and Martí.[57]

According to Ivan Schulman, Martí was like Emerson in his implicit preference for symbols of nature. Schulman points to light, sun, and star as three major symbols used by both Emerson and Martí.[58] This critic finds evidence of Emerson's concept of analogies in nature being incorporated into Martí's thinking, and while he notes that the idea of harmonious conciliation may have come to Martí through Spanish followers of the German philosopher Karl C. F. Krause, he believes that the major influence was Emerson.[59] In Schulman's view, Martí's symbolic theory does not include Emerson's concept of linguistic fluidity but does stress the Emersonian doctrine of constant ascension to a higher form.[60] He also shows how both Emerson and Martí recognized the validity of analogy in regard to sound and color.[61]

As writers Emerson and Martí cultivated similar forms. Both composed chiefly essays and poetry, and both wrote discourses and letters of literary quality. Both the North American and the Spanish American kept notebooks in which they recorded thoughts, inspirations, and explanations. And as critics both were discerning, yet somewhat indulgent of friends and contemporaries.

Repetition, illustration, and the use of examples are characteristic of both Emerson's and Martí's essays. At times, too, each author seemed to bound from thought to thought in an attempt to get everything said at once and lose nothing. Further, Martí seemed to believe that the method by which he thought, gathered inspiration, and created was the same as Emerson's method. Both men excelled in creating maxims that are widely quoted, and each has enjoyed a substantial and sustained influence in his own cultural world. Martí is recognized today as one of the principal figures in the renovation in Spanish letters known as *modernismo*. Similarly, Emerson exerted an extraordinary influence on writers, both American and foreign. In literary stature the two are decidedly equals, a link that doubtless would have pleased Martí.

Emerson's Thought in Martí

Students of Martí and Emerson have found similarities between the two, an Emersonian influence in *Versos sencillos*, and evidence of Emerson's influence on Martí in the realm of conceptual thinking. Some believe that Hindu thinking may have come to Martí chiefly through Emerson. Others see Martí's thought as combining elements of German idealism, received through Krause and Emerson, with elements of positivism, received through Herbert Spencer.[62] Yet another line of thought claims that though there is much transcendentalism in Martí's thought, the Cuban writer's philosophical outlook was basically fixed by the time he came into contact with Emerson.[63]

Emerson's influence on Martí's conceptual thinking is diffused yet discernable. Two examples of concepts that likely flowed from Emerson to Martí are, in very general terms, the concept of analogies in nature and the concept of constant ascension to a higher form. The concept of analogies could have come from Emerson, from Krause, or from both, but if interest is an indicator, then Emerson is the more likely influence, since Martí wrote far more about Emerson than about Krause. As for the concept of continuing ascension to a higher form, Emerson's influence on Martí is highly probable. As noted earlier, the lines "And, striving to be man, the worm / Mounts through all the spires of form" (21:408) appear to have fascinated Martí and are recorded at several points in his writing. Martí felt that Emerson's verses foreshadowed the theory of evolution, and this bolstered his belief in the importance of the poet.

A greater, yet more subtle, Emerson influence on Martí exists in the form of inspiration. Emerson's moral example, his confidence, and his trust in nature converged as a beacon of hope for Martí—an assurance expressed in the "afternoon of Emerson" of Martí's notes. Quite likely, Emerson's greatest impact on Martí was not on his writing or on his "philosophy" but on his life. What is certain is that, in Emerson, Martí found a kindred soul.

Conclusions

Martí's work on Emerson was enduring and heartfelt. The American author was a topic in Martí's writing from 1881 until at least 1890, and the material that the Cuban took from Emerson came from throughout the American author's works. The major essay about Emerson featured twenty-three allusions to *Nature* and references to passages in "The Over-Soul," "Montaigne; or, the Skeptic," "Self-Reliance," and the poem "Wealth." The quotations and references alone indicate a wide range of reading, and this, together with the understanding of Emerson that Martí displayed throughout his writing, confirms that his knowledge about Emerson was substantial.

Martí was anxious to share this knowledge and made Emerson a part of nearly all of his writing. He composed a powerful essay to honor Emerson's memory, sang his praises in continuous references in his articles, jotted down quotations and ideas from Emerson, mentioned him in correspondence, featured him in *La Edad de Oro*, and translated his verses. No other American author was so reverently treated and so extensively portrayed.

Martí and Whitman

Revolutionary Minds

The robust voice of America's revolutionary poet Walt Whitman first reached a Latin American readership through José Martí. Today, Whitman is championed throughout the Americas, his celebratory verses subject to multiple readings, and his impact extensively registered. Many authors have laid claim to Whitman's legacy: Jorge Luis Borges, Pablo Neruda, Octavio Paz, José Lezama Lima, the Dominican national poet Pedro Mir, and others.[1] But it was Martí who first brought Whitman's words to the Southern Hemisphere.

The Cuban chronicler introduced Whitman to "his America" through essay and comments much the way that he had profiled Emerson. Martí's writing on Whitman includes brief commentaries plus a major essay and spans the years of his exile in the United States. As early as 1881, Martí featured comments on Whitman in his articles, and in 1887 he published an essay honoring the American poet in both *El Partido Liberal* and *La Nación*. This essay was written following Whitman's Lincoln Lecture in New York in April 1887, a lecture Martí very likely attended, and is Martí's most important analysis and assessment of the Poet of Democracy.

At least five translations of the essay are available in English. In their collections of Martí's writings Juan de Onís, Luis Baralt, and Esther Allen have all published English versions that have enjoyed wide distribution. In each case the translator went directly to Whitman's works to find sources for what Martí had expressed in Spanish. Baralt provided complete documentation for the Whitman quotations and included more than forty references to Whitman in his notes on the translation.[2]

The Essay on Whitman

Opening his 1887 tribute to Whitman with a pictorial depiction—"He seemed like a god last night, seated in his red velvet chair, with flowing white hair, beard down to his chest, eyebrows as thick as a forest and his hand on a staff" (13:131)—Martí continued with a description of the seventy-year-old poet as a master of prophetic language who wrote poetry with vigorous strokes and maxims that burst forth with energy and wisdom. This Whitman, writer of astounding and prohibited lines, appreciated by only the most discerning critics, was presented by Martí as one who merited special ranking in his nation's literary history.

Martí explained that weak and petty men were unable to accept Whitman's embrace, for such small-minded men sought differences rather than accepting concepts common to mankind. They fled before Whitman's directness and his encompassing and powerful presence. With Whitman, as with Emerson, Martí insisted that the detractors were trapped by their own shortcomings and thus failed to appreciate natural greatness.

Martí emphasized the Whitmanesque qualities of originality, vigor, and uncompromising humanity. He praised Whitman's style and method and named some of the American writer's works. Martí's article indulged in extensive borrowing from Whitman—letting the author speak for himself to the readers. The essay included numerous quotations and paraphrases from throughout Whitman's writing but contained only passing reference to the author's life.

The Martí essay on Whitman, much like the one on Emerson, made use of a pattern in which Martí's comments alternated with the words of the author he described. For example, after explaining the impression that Whitman's poetry created, Martí included quotations from the American author's poems. After referring to the Lincoln Lecture, he recorded lines from Whitman's poetry on Lincoln.

The first Whitman work that Martí touched on was *Leaves of Grass*, which initially was not named but alluded to only as a "prohibited" text (13:131). A scant two paragraphs into Martí's essay, lines from *Leaves of Grass* began to appear in translation. Martí translated or paraphrased many lines from Whitman, and a careful correlation of these lines with the original verses reveals how closely Martí relied on the poet's own words.

Walt Whitman, June 1887. Courtesy of the Library of Congress, Prints and Photographs Division (LC-USZ62-106847).

In sharing the poet with his readers, Martí began (13:132) by confirming the fame and stature of Whitman with his "persona natural,"[3] his "naturaleza sin freno en original energía,"[4] his "miríadas de mancebos hermosos y gigantes,"[5] his belief that "el más breve retoño demuestra que en realidad no hay muerte,"[6] and his determination to "callar mientras los demás discuten e ir a bañarse y a admirarse a sí mismo, conociendo la perfecta propiedad y armonía de las cosas."[7] Martí presented the American poet as "el que no dice estas poesías por un peso,"[8] who "está satisfecho, y ve, baila, canta y ríe,"[9] and who "no tiene cátedra, ni púlpito, ni escuela."[10]

Whitman merited study, Martí said. Emerson, Tennyson, and Robert Buchanan had all praised him. Then the Cuban writer returned to Whitman's poetry. "El lee en el ojo del buey y en la savia de la hoja,"[11] Martí said, and then quoted: "¡Ese que limpia suciedades de vuestra casa, ése es mi hermano!" (13:132).[12] Whitman did not live, Martí reported with further quotes, in his "Manhattan querida,"[13] in his "Manhattan de rostro soberbio y un millón de pies,"[14] where he appeared when he wanted to intone "el canto de lo que ve a la Libertad" (13:132).[15] He lived, said Martí, cared for by "loving friends"; he loved to see the "strong young men," the "camaradas." Describing Whitman as an iconoclast who wanted to establish "la institución de la camaradería" (13:133),[16] Martí translated these lines: "Ni orgías, ni ostentosas paradas, ni la continua procesión de las calles, ni las ventanas atestadas de comercios, ni la conversación con los eruditos me satisface, sino que al pasar por mi Manhattan los ojos que encuentra me ofrezcan amor; amantes, continuos amantes es lo único que me satisface" (13:133).[17] He then compared Whitman to the old men "announced" at the end of Leaves of Grass—"Anuncio miríadas de mancebos gigantescos, hermosos y de fina sangre; anuncio una raza de ancianos salvajes y espléndidos"—and continued quoting from Whitman with "los gañanes que charlan a la merienda sobre las pilas de ladrillos, la ambulancia que corre desalada con el héroe que acaba de caerse de un andamio, la mujer sorprendida en medio de la turba por la fatiga augusta de la maternidad" (13:133).[18]

Martí turned to the theme of Lincoln's death and to Whitman's poetry on "aquella poderosa estrella muerta del Oeste" (13:133).[19] He described the haunting beauty of "When Lilacs Last in the Dooryard Bloom'd" and gave a quotation from Whitman about death: "la cosecha, la que abre la puerta, la gran reveladora" (13:134).[20]

With the proclamation "Listen to Walt Whitman" Martí introduced a series of quotations and paraphrases: "Lo infinitésimo colabora para lo infinito, y todo está en su puesto, la tortuga, el buey, los pájaros, 'propósitos alados'";[21] "Tanta fortuna es morir como nacer, porque los muertos están vivos";[22] "Nadie puede decir lo tranquilo que está él sobre Dios y la muerte!";[23] "Se ríe de lo que llaman desilusión, y conoce la amplitud del tiempo; él acepta absolutamente el tiempo";[24] "En su persona se contiene todo: todo él está en todo; donde uno se degrada, él se degrada; él es la marea, el flujo y reflujo";[25] "¿Qué le importa a él volver al seno de donde partió, y convertirse al amor de la tierra húmeda, en vegetal útil, en flor bella?" (13:136).[26]

Martí wrote that in "Song of Myself" Whitman said of the animals that "ninguno se arrodilla ante otro, ni es superior al otro, ni se queja,"[27] then from the same poem he quoted: "ya se ha denunciado y tonteado bastante" (13:136–37).[28] Whitman was "de todas las castas, credos y profesiones";[29] Whitman instructed doctor and priest to leave the sick man alone, saying: "yo me apegaré a él, abriré las ventanas, le amaré, le hablaré al oído; ya veréis cómo sana; vosotros sois palabra y yerba, pero yo puedo más que vosotros porque soy amor";[30] Whitman called the Creator "el verdadero amante, el camarada perfecto" (13:137).[31]

How could Whitman's vast and ardent love be expressed? Martí let the author of *Leaves of Grass*—which Martí translated as *Hojas de Yerba*—speak for himself: "Yo haré ilustres . . . las palabras y las ideas que los hombres han prostituido con su sigilo y su falsa vergüenza; yo canto y consagro lo que consagraba el Egipto"[32] and "¡mi deber es crear!"[33] and "Yo canto al cuerpo eléctrico" (13:137–38).[34]

To demonstrate the tenderness as well as the vitality of Whitman's treatment of love, Martí translated two brief poems, "Beautiful Women" and "Mother and Babe." The first was a direct and straightforward translation: "Las mujeres se sientan o se mueven de un lado para otro, jóvenes algunas, algunas viejas; las jóvenes son hermosas, pero las viejas son más hermosas que las jóvenes";[35] the second was in the form of a paraphrase: "Ve el niño que duerme, el niño: ¡silencio! Los estudió largamente" (13:138).[36]

Martí showed that Whitman was open to all the senses. He repeated Whitman's appeal "¡penétrame, oh mar, de humedad amorosa!"[37] and explained that Whitman wanted doors without locks and bodies in their natural beauty: "cree que santifica cuanto toca o le toca, y halla virtud a todo lo corpóreo" (13:138).[38] And he presented the poet in the poet's own bold words: "'Walt Whitman, un cosmos, el hijo de Manhattan, turbulento, sensual, carnoso, que come, bebe y engendra, ni más ni menos que todos los demás" (13:138).[39]

Martí paraphrased Whitman's poem "A Clear Midnight": "Pero cuando en la clara medianoche, libre el alma de ocupaciones y de libros, emerge entera, silenciosa y contemplativa del día noblemente empleado, medita en los temas que más la complacen: en la noche, el sueño y la muerte . . ." (13:138).[40] A little later he quoted Whitman's thought that "es muy dulce morir avanzando" (13:139).[41]

Among the many paraphrased thoughts in the essay, especially from "Song of Myself," which Martí called "Canto de mí mismo," are: "Pero sólo a las olas del océano halla dignas de corear, a la luz de la luna, su dicha al ver dormido junto a sí al amigo que ama";[42] "Echa el brazo por el hombro a los carreros, a los marineros, a los labradores. Caza y pesca con ellos, y en la siega sube con ellos al tope del carro cargado";[43] "Más bello que un emperador triunfante le parece el negro vigoroso que, apoyado en la lanza detrás de sus percherones, guía su carro sereno por el revuelto Broadway";[44] "Siente un placer heroico cuando se detiene en el umbral de una herrería y ve que los mancebos con el torso desnudo, revuelan por sobre sus cabezas los martillos, y dan cada uno a su turno";[45] "Cuando el esclavo llega a sus puertas perseguido y sudoroso, le llena la bañadera, lo sienta a su mesa; en el rincón tiene cargada la escopeta para defenderlo; si se lo vienen a atacar, matará a su perseguidor y volverá a sentarse a la mesa, ¡como si hubiera matado una víbora!" (13:139).[46]

Martí continued with more quotations. He said that Whitman had cast aside romantic laments: "¡no he de pedirle al cielo que baje a la Tierra para hacer mi voluntad!" (13:139).[47] In Martí's pages, Whitman spoke to scientists: "Vosotros sois los primeros . . . pero la ciencia no es más que un departamento de mi morada, no es toda mi morada" (13:140).[48] He declared: "¡qué pobres parecen las argucias ante un hecho heroico!"[49] and "A la ciencia salve, y salve el alma, que está por sobre toda la ciencia"[50] and "Aquel que cerca de mí muestra un pecho más ancho que el mío, demuestra la anchura del mío" (13:140).[51] He revealed his connection to nature: "Penetre el Sol la Tierra, hasta toda ella sea luz clara y dulce como mi sangre. Sea universal el goce. Yo canto la eternidad de la existencia, la dicha de nuestra vida y la hermosura implacable del Universo. Yo uso zapato de Becerro, un cuello espacioso y un bastón hecho de una rama de árbol" (13:140).[52]

Near the end of the essay Martí again indicated that Whitman's voice should be heard. He had Whitman himself say how he spoke: "en alaridos proféticos";[53] "éstas son . . . unas pocas palabras indicadoras de lo futuro";[54] "di, Tierra, viejo nudo montuoso, ¿qué quieres de mí?";[55] "hago resonar mi bárbara fanfarria sobre los techos del mundo" (13:141).[56] Martí closed his essay with the same words Whitman had used to close *Leaves of Grass*: he described Whitman living out his later years sure in the belief that after death he would return "¡desembarazado, triunfante, muerto!" (13:143).[57]

The translations and paraphrases cited make clear that Martí's familiarity with Whitman's poetry was extensive and that he wanted those reading his chronicles to have direct access to the poet's words. Altogether Martí offered nearly seventy phrases and/or lines from Whitman in his essay. He named *Calamus* and *Children of Adam* as collections of works and "Salut au Monde," "Song of Myself," "I Sing the Body Electric," "Beautiful Women," and "Mother and Babe" as individual poems.

Martí wrote approvingly of Whitman's style, asserting that the irregularity of his verse was only apparent, not real (13:132). A revolutionary in both politics and poetry himself, Martí praised Whitman's bold strophes, finding them well suited to the vigorous life of the new continent. He saw in Whitman's language a rhythm dependent not on rhymes and accents but on the robust construction of stanzas where the poet played out his ideas in magnificent musical phrases. Martí claimed that this was the natural poetic form for a people who built by tremendous blocks, rather than stone by stone (13:140).

If Whitman's language seemed strange, it was a good match for the power and panorama of his message. The Cuban writer explained that polite versification and delicate themes were inadequate for the description of a colossal and ambitious nation (13:140–41). In writing of *Calamus*, Martí defended Whitman's forceful, direct, and corporeal language and chided those who saw in the lines a reflection of homosexual love. Yet even as he championed the Whitmanesque depiction of love in *Calamus*, Martí was un-Whitman-like in his response. He resorted to classical allusions to distance Whitman from homoerotic instincts, disparaging those "who believed they found in Whitman's ardent praise of the love between friends, a return to Virgil's vile desire for Cebetes or Horace's for Gyges and Lyciscus" (13:137).

Martí cast the author of *Children of Adam* as virile, and as a man who took satisfaction in enumerating the parts of a woman's body, "like a hungry hero, smacking his sanguine lips," yet he emphasized that Whitman was not brutal and was unusual in his ability to combine virility and tenderness (13:138).

Martí's commentary on Whitman's style became most specific in treating "When Lilacs Last in the Dooryard Bloom'd," which he called "one of the most beautiful creations of contemporary poetry" (13:134). He showed how the clouds, the stars and moon, and the solitary thrush all contributed to the melancholy mood of the poem; how nature accompanied the journey of the coffin; and how the earth itself seemed to join in the mourning. It is not evident that Martí fully appreciated the symbol of the lilac. All he said was: "The poet brings a sprig of lilac to the coffin" (13:134). Martí compared this poem to "The Raven" by Edgar Allan Poe and said that Whitman's "mystic threnody" was much more beautiful, strange, and profound (13:134).

How did the American writer approach his task? What was his method? According to Martí, Whitman created his own grammar and logic (13:132). His strategy was to reproduce the various elements of a composition in the same "disorder" in which they appeared in nature. Whitman did not compare, but his descriptions were graphic and incisive. All contributed to a masterful impression of the whole (13:141). For Martí, all Whitman needed to stretch or to shrink a phrase was an adverb; all he needed to reinforce a line was an adjective. Whitman's revolutionary method might seem no method at all, but the effect was great. Said Martí of Whitman's use of words: "he combines [them] with unheard-of audacity, putting august and almost divine words next to others that seem the least appropriate and decent" (13:142).[58] Martí maintained that Whitman painted with sounds arranged with consummate skill and carefully juggled arrangements—lest a reader's interest lag. And Martí wrote of Whitman's ability to bring forth melancholy from repetition and to describe by accumulation, including borrowed words from Spanish, French, and Italian (13:142).

The words and symbols Martí employed in his essay shed light on his interpretation of Whitman. He compared Whitman's works to the composition of mountains (13:132); he said that Whitman knew universal greatness (13:139) and that he sowed eagles (13:141). But Whitman's works were also characterized as strange, startling, and daring. Martí left his readers with an impression about Whitman that was built around strong words: natural, robust, intrepid, bold, strange, forceful. This stands in contrast to Martí's reverential treatment of Emerson and highlights the different degrees of esteem in which Martí held the two authors.

Martí's Whitman was astonishing and impressive; Martí's Emerson was victorious and triumphant. Martí respected Whitman's revolutionary stance but saw in Emerson a kindred soul. Nowhere is the difference between the two essays—and the two assessments—more evident than in the manner in which each article opened and closed. Martí's Emerson accolade began with the writer tremulous at the very thought of his task and ended with a glowing personal tribute. The Whitman essay, in contrast, opened with a newspaper account and closed with words from the American poet.

References in Articles and Notes

The brief references to Whitman in Martí's works can be grouped into three basic categories: entries that appeared before the 1887 essay, commentary that appeared after the 1887 essay, and unpublished references including notebook comments and notes in correspondence. Of these the pre-1887 category is the most significant.

Martí's first allusion to Whitman appeared in print on November 15, 1881. It was for the "Sección Constante" column of *La Opinión Nacional* and identified the poet simply as "W." Here Martí wrote that the author was directing the publication of his collected works in Boston and was known for bold rhymes, daring thoughts, and a lack of restraint—bordering on disrespect—in form (13:81). In December of the same year, Martí said that the preponderance of news about Garfield's assassin had overshadowed the verses of Walt Whitman, verses Martí described as "great and irregular like mountains" (9:132). In another 1881 reference, Martí related Whitman's visit to the gravesides of Hawthorne and Thoreau, where the "rebellious poet" took a stone from the ground and placed it on the small mountain of stones left by visitors to the two graves (23:128). Martí described Whitman as one who "sings of heaven's domain and nature's marvels in a language replete with tenderness and shades of moonlight and who celebrates with the nakedness of spring and, at times, with prolific boldness, the coarse and lustful forces of mankind." Continuing the contrast, Martí said that Whitman painted "red things as very red and faint things as very faint" (23:128).

In his December 1882 letter to the director of *La Nación*, Martí had suggested that U.S. authors who remained to be studied included Henry James and a vigorous and rebellious poet named Walt Whitman (9:18). Yet until the 1887 essay, Martí made only one allusion to Whitman in his articles for *La Nación*. That passing comment appeared in an article published June 6, 1884, where Martí chronicled the campaign by Harvard students to make English rather than Latin the official language of the university. The students, said Martí, preferred the language in which Irving sketched colors and in which Whitman was creating mountains of waves (10:47).

Another reference of 1884 was published in *La América*, where Martí wrote that although Whittier, Holmes, and Lowell were still living, the United States had no real poet left—since Sidney Lanier had died—except for Walt Whitman, an admirable rebel who could break a branch in the forest and find poetry in it (8:427–28). Martí's additional comment described Whitman as eschewing the rumpled texts and formal trappings of academe and of belonging to only one academy—that of nature.

Martí made several brief references to Whitman after the 1887 essay, but not a single one appeared in *La Nación* and not one contributed significantly to acquainting Spanish Americans with Whitman. In 1888 Martí referred in passing to Whitman in an article for *El Economista Americano*, commenting that the poetic soul had pursued beauty from the times of Homer to Whitman (5:138). In 1889 in *La Opinión Pública* of Montevideo, Martí included a line about every college student carrying a copy of Walt Whitman (12:306). The September 27, 1889, issue of *El Partido Liberal* carried a Martí article that said: "'Libertad' is such a beautiful and honest word that Walt Whitman, the patriarchal poet of the North, never says it in English, but the way he learned it from the Mexicans" (7: 351). Martí also mentioned Whitman in *Patria*: in the May 21, 1892, edition he offered the examples of Victor Hugo and Walt Whitman as two authors who kept their hearts closely attuned to everyday people and everyday life. Martí described Whitman as the most native and powerful of the U.S. poets and one who spent long hours talking to coachmen on Broadway, those men who saw the complete book of life pass before their eyes each day (1:451).

Martí's notes feature few references to Whitman. He is mentioned along with Emerson, Carlyle, Motley, and Longfellow for inclusion in what Martí called "Mi libro" (18:286) and was listed again for inclusion under the heading "Mi libro. Los poetas rebeldes" (18:283). In another notebook entry a single line reads: "the verse of W. Whitman—whose beard curls" (21:279). A letter to Manuel Mercado records an additional reference. Martí was complaining of errors in his writing published by *El Partido Liberal* and said: "I know that my poor handwriting is to blame, but the gentlemen who set type will understand that I love men as Walt Whitman does and they will forgive me" (20:132).

Similarities and Differences

Martí and Whitman were both revolutionary voices in their own cultural worlds; both were innovative in letters and both preferred natural verse forms and a lack of artifice. Both wrote with deep humanitarian and democratic instincts and both were invigorated by the possibility of new poetry in a new hemisphere. Both Martí and Whitman envisioned poetry as essentially "inspired" and spontaneous, rather than constrained and preconceived. The two writers shared a generalized conception of immortality, and both were independent yet confident of their craft.[59]

Differences between Martí and Whitman are also marked. The Cuban writer, by turns a motivator, a diplomat, and a man under pressure to persuade, was incapable of Whitman's candor. Martí's treatment of love was restrained, and he used the power of suggestion to convey passion. Whitman was overtly physical and direct. Martí repeatedly employed the word "strange" in writing of Whitman, an adjective he hardly would have wished for himself. And while Martí admired the American author's originality and spirit of rebellion, he maintained a distance from Whitman.

A contrast of Martí/Emerson and Martí/Whitman underscores the differences between Martí and Whitman. Martí and Emerson both found refuge in countryside tranquility and wrote poems praising an escape from urban activity. Whitman, on the other hand, loved the press of bodies and the jostle of life in Manhattan. Furthermore, Martí showed intense personal involvement while writing of Emerson and a degree of detachment when describing Whitman.

Conclusions

Martí's appreciation of Whitman's rebellious voice contrasts with the tepid reception Whitman received from some of the prominent critics of the era and confirms the wisdom of the Cuban's literary critique.[60] Martí portrayed Whitman as a vigorous and original poet. He emphasized the force and grandeur of Whitman's writing and clearly approved of his democratic and humanitarian values. The Cuban writer considered Whitman one of America's greatest authors and presented a candid and comprehensive sampling of Whitman's work in the 1887 essay.

Martí's essay with its many translations and paraphrases of Whitman's poetry was a principal way in which Spanish Americans were introduced to the author of *Leaves of Grass,* and Martí is acknowledged as an important link between Whitman and Latin America. One immediate example of the impact of Martí's writing is the case of Rubén Darío, the Nicaraguan who played a major role in the late-nineteenth-century revolution in Spanish letters with his "modernist" prose and poetry. Darío paid tribute to Whitman in his verses and acknowledged that he had first learned of the author of *Leaves of Grass* thanks to Martí.[61]

Martí and Longfellow

The Mellifluous Voice

The mellifluous voice of Henry Wadsworth Longfellow produced Martí's first published comment about a U.S. writer. In Mexico, in an April 1875 article for the *Revista Universal*, Martí called Longfellow an eminent and pleasing singer of verses, a man with a generous heart, and a creator of original legends and poems that were sometimes delicate but always profound. Martí hailed Longfellow as a son of the American continent who sang along with nature and whose fresh, robust verses resounded like waves of a river. He mentioned the delicious, primitive flavor of *Hiawatha* and the depth of sentiment and tenderness of *Evangeline*. Martí began the brief commentary by reporting a visit to Mexico by Longfellow's son and closed by saying that Mexico welcomed the son because of the goodwill that the father's works inspired.[1] Writing for the *Revista Universal* in September of 1875, Martí told Mexican readers that the first edition of a new Longfellow poem had sold out completely. Here Martí praised Longfellow's lyrical voice and said that the poet's merit set him apart from the nation where he lived.[2] Then in 1877, in a prospectus for a magazine about Guatemala, Martí again alluded to Longfellow.[3] In the prospectus, Martí praised Guatemala's reserve of natural resources, reminding his prospective public that at one time such extraordinary and fertile lands were untapped in North America. Martí referred to those times as an era when the first Christian prayer was raised heavenward from Plymouth and the only salvos were the sorrowful laments of Hiawatha (7:105).

Martí's appreciation of Longfellow very likely began in Havana under the tutelage of his boyhood mentor Rafael María de Mendive, who is believed to have read and studied Longfellow. Mendive was a poet, cultivated a love of literature in his students, and read and translated English and American authors. And the library in Mendive's school included a book by Longfellow inscribed by the poet.[4]

Martí's early acquaintance with Longfellow is confirmed by the fact that the poet's name appeared in Martí's very first New York chronicles. In the third of the "Impressions of America by a very fresh Spaniard," published in the *Hour* in 1880, Martí made reference to the "charming melody" of Longfellow (19:122). Although he mentioned other English-language authors in the article, the only U.S. writer Martí referred to was Longfellow.

Articles about Longfellow

Martí published his first full article about Longfellow in *La Opinión Nacional* on March 22, 1882. President Garfield had just died and Martí wrote that now the nation's esteemed poet was near death's door: "A cancer gnaws at the face of Longfellow, who four days ago completed his seventy-fifth year" (13:225). The readers of *La Opinión Nacional* learned how the United States paid homage to a revered writer. In Atlanta, children both black and white recited lines from "Excelsior." In Atlanta, Cambridge, and Boston, not a child's hand was without flowers, nor a child's lips without verse, and throughout the land, admirers proclaimed "Excelsior!" (13:225).

In Martí's introduction of Longfellow he described the poet's home and life as well as his poetry. Longfellow's home in Cambridge had served as headquarters for General Washington during part of the Revolutionary War, and the American author was proud of this heritage.[5] Martí's article evoked both the historical legacy and the aesthetic qualities of the house, surrounding Longfellow with an aura of American history while placing him in a comfortable setting. The Cuban patriot praised the bravery of the stubborn revolutionaries who defended nearby Bunker Hill; he wrote that Longfellow told time by a clock that Washington had used; and he asserted that the poet "encased and set his polished rhymes" in a room where Washington had worked out battle plans (13:225). Martí described the drawing room with its wide chimney framed by China vases and rich with ornamentation and wrote that Longfellow worked at a round table set with books (13:226).

Henry Wadsworth Longfellow. Courtesy of the Library of Congress, Prints and Photographs Division (LC-USZ62-103577).

Longfellow's "charmed" life intrigued Martí, who described the poet's career as one of good fortune and tranquility. He mentioned Longfellow's work as Harvard professor and teacher of languages and considered him a worthy successor to George Ticknor, who like Longfellow had taught at Harvard and studied the Spanish classics. In addition, Martí wrote approvingly of Longfellow's travel to Europe to gain firsthand knowledge of language and literature (13:225–27).

Martí gave the titles (in Spanish) of several Longfellow works— *Voices of the Night, Birds of Passage, Ballads, Evangeline, Hiawatha,* and

Tales of a Wayside Inn—following each with brief words of explanation or description. He also mentioned Longfellow's translations from Lope de Vega and Jorge Manrique and praised the bard's gift for sensing the music of other tongues and expressing with a sure touch the literature of other lands (13:226).

How did Martí portray the poet's art? He called Longfellow's verses fresh, gentle, and serene, and described their effect as soothing and consoling. Martí appreciated Longfellow's success in harvesting "some of the most beautiful flowers of a new orchard" (13:226) and his ability to give voice to "profound thoughts in winged verses" (13:227).[6] And he called him a nightingale of verse, who painted with colors rather than ink, and who had discovered perfection of form (13:227).

Martí, who experienced betrayal in his personal life and anguish over the future of his fatherland, believed that poems often spring from a poet's despair; the prologue to *Versos sencillos* establishes this very link. In the Longfellow piece Martí stated, "Pain nurtures poetry" (13:227), and implied—but without saying so directly—that Longfellow had not suffered sufficiently to produce mature poetry: "He speaks of faith in an age when so many speak of desperation. His verses release a beautiful sadness, the blue sadness of one who has not suffered" (13:227). Martí also said of Longfellow that the angels who inspired him had wings untouched by blood (13:227), and that the slings of misfortune had been turned away from his home (13:228).

Was Martí aware of the personal tragedies in Longfellow's life: the death of both of his wives, the second burned to death in 1861? Did Martí realize that the "nightingale of verse" had suffered grievous burns trying to save a beloved spouse and that the sonnet written eighteen years after this loss, "The Cross of Snow," was one of Longfellow's best poems?[7] Apparently not, for the Cuban writer makes no mention of these sorrows. It is possible, however, that Martí meant merely to emphasize the fullness of Longfellow's long life—a fine home, loving children, many friends, literary success, and the affection and appreciation of his countrymen.

Martí's second tribute to Longfellow was written following the poet's death. The article was dated April 1, 1882, and appeared just ten days later in *La Opinión Nacional*.

Martí began by saying that the celebrated poet was "at rest" and proclaimed his own mourning. "Longfellow has died. Oh how the good poets keep us company! What tender friends even when we do not know them! What benefactors those who sing of things divine and console us! They may make us cry, but how they ease the pain!" (13:228). Whether consciously or unconsciously, Martí's emphatic lines were the perfect poetic register for lamenting Longfellow's death. The American author had translated an eloquent elegy from Medieval Spanish literature, the "Coplas on the Death of His Father" by Jorge Manrique, and Martí's bold proclamations of sorrow echo lines from the "Coplas." Then, with loving attention to detail, Martí described the interment.

Martí's portrait of Longfellow placed the beloved poet in a framework of harmony and beauty. Peace, loveliness, and virtue filled the poet's days. His study of European languages and literatures had expanded and enlightened his thinking. Yet Longfellow's poetic light was strong and sure, never blinded by the reflection of other lights. And Martí dismissed the carping of critics with these words: "Crows croaked at him the way that crows always croak at eagles" (13:229). Was Martí referring to Edgar Allan Poe as one of the "crows" who criticized the "eagle" Longfellow with scant justification? Did Martí associate the author of "The Raven" with the word "cuervo," which means both raven and crow in Spanish? There is no way to be sure, but this comment on literary criticism at least suggests an indirect reference to Poe.

In this article Martí compared Longfellow's verses to "sonorous urns" and "Greek statues," perfect in proportion and harmony, and described the poetry as a "vase of myrrh from which the fragrant essence of mankind could ascend in homage" (13:229).

Martí appreciated Longfellow's thematic diversity. "Finns, Norwegians, Salamancan students, Moravian nuns, Swedish ghosts, picturesque colonial scenes, and Native America" all figured in his writing (13:229). But for the Cuban, Longfellow's poems of spiritual exaltation and communion with nature were his best (13:229–30). In describing the author's "long and tender dialogues with nature" (13:229–30), Martí used the archaism "luengo" for "long," a usage that enhanced the melancholy mood and seemed especially apt for an American writer familiar with old Spanish.

Martí connected the tranquility of Longfellow's life with the idealism of his works and cited "Excelsior" as an example. "Life to him was a mountain: to be alive involved the obligation of carrying a white banner to its summit" (13:230).[8] Martí also appreciated the repose in which

Longfellow lived and alluded to the shade of the chestnut tree in the poem "The Village Blacksmith."

Martí lingered over memories associated with Longfellow. He mentioned the armchair made from the wood of the Village Blacksmith's chestnut tree—an armchair given to Longfellow by the children of Cambridge (13:230). And he mentioned the old grandfather clock on the stairs in the Longfellow home. According to Martí, this was the clock referred to in the poem "The Old Clock on the Stairs" and the same clock that General Washington had watched when he used the house for his headquarters (13:230).[9]

In describing the burial, Martí contrasted the biblical words "dust thou art, and unto dust shalt thou return" spoken by the poet's brother with the lines from Longfellow's poem "A Psalm of Life": "Dust thou art, to dust returnest, / Was not spoken of the soul" (13:230).[10] Finally Martí listed literary figures who had attended the funeral: Holmes, Curtis, Howells, Whittier, and Emerson (13:230–31).

Martí's message in these two articles on Longfellow was consistent. Longfellow was a gentle, kind, and good poet who composed pleasing and comforting lines and created harmonious works of art. Longfellow's life was compared to a murmuring brook that refreshed his feet and brought him flowers (13:225). And Martí portrayed Longfellow's death as serene, like a wave absorbed by the sea (13:230).

References in Articles and Notes

Many of Martí's references to Longfellow appeared in the "Sección Constante" column he wrote for *La Opinión Nacional*. These references covered the range of the American author's work. In November of 1881, in writing about the southern poet Paul Hamilton Hayne, Martí observed that Hayne was to the "impassioned Creoles" of the South as Longfellow was to the North (23:69). In a January 1882 column, Martí described the U.S. custom of publishing "birthday" editions of famous writers' works and noted that Longfellow—who certainly was deserving—had been paid this honor (23:178).

By May of 1882, Martí dedicated nearly half of his commentary for the "Sección Constante" to Longfellow, recounting the sale of the poem "The Hanging of the Crane" to the *New York Ledger*. Martí did not name either the poem or the newspaper but stated that a New York paper had paid the poet four thousand dollars for the privilege of printing one of his poems. The purchase was justified, Martí explained, because the poem told a beautiful story and was composed with a fine touch. And, he continued, its music was pleasing to the ear, its art was pleasing to the mind, and its chaste and melancholy sadness pleased the heart (23:302–3). "Beauty alleviates," said Martí, and "A beautiful song is a good deed: he who gives guests to the heart, provides companions for life's sorrows" (23:303). Martí concluded with the thought that poetry outlasts empires: "Troy is in ruins," he wrote, "not the *Iliad*" (23:303).

"The Hanging of the Crane," which takes its name from the installation of a chimney crane in the home of a young couple, is a light piece of poetry and is not considered one of Longfellow's best works. It tells the story of a married couple from their days as newlyweds to their golden anniversary. Martí took delight in describing this "ideal home": the preparation of the house, the ambience of the table for which the husband provided food and the wife cheerfulness, the joys of raising children, the departure of sons and daughters grown up and moved away, and the renewed happiness brought by grandchildren (23:303). Martí was successful in transmitting the consoling effect of these scenes and presented the poem as gratifying—if not great.

In other comments for *La Opinión Nacional*, Martí explained the title of the Longfellow work "Ultima Thule" by quoting verses from Seneca about the Utmost Isle (23:191). In a reference written shortly after Longfellow's death, Martí noted several of the American author's poems and said that Longfellow was widely translated but that one of his finest pieces of poetry, "Morituri Salutamus," had not yet been put into Spanish. He described "Morituri Salutamus," a poem Longfellow wrote for the fiftieth anniversary of his college class, as a "code of life" that was good reading for both young and old; he hailed "Excelsior" as "a true song of the human struggle"; he listed "A Psalm of Life," "The Rainy Day," "The Light of Stars," "The Skeleton in Armor," "The Village Blacksmith," and "The Old Clock on the Stairs" as poems "of poignant tenderness and virile melancholy" (23:273).

In addition to the "Sección Constante" comments, Martí made passing reference to Longfellow in listings of authors and in association with Boston and Massachusetts. Like Emerson, Longfellow was often linked to the writers and writing of New England. For example, an 1884 article for the New York paper *La América* described Longfellow as "the melodious and serene poet who took the harsh sounds of English and forged from them a smooth, perfect, and sonorous language" (8:427).

In two instances Martí commented on works or characters rather than on Longfellow himself. For an 1888 article sent to *La Nación*, he described a walking marathon held in New York and alluded to quick-footed figures of legend and literature, including Pau-Puk-Keewis who danced at Hiawatha's wedding feast. He paraphrased lines from *The Song of Hiawatha*, portraying the Indian's attire as "camisa y calzoneras de piel de venado con pasamanería de wampunes de colores, y diadema de plumas de cisne" (11:401).[11] He also included a recounting of the poem "Excelsior" in a romantic dialogue between two of the characters in his novel *Amistad funesta* (18:239).

Martí referred to Longfellow in his notebooks in ways that reflected his comments in print. Longfellow was listed along with other American authors such as Whitman and Emerson, and in a notation of the title "Ultima Thule" (22:116). Elsewhere in the notes Martí expressed his belief that suffering gave birth to poetic ideas, and at the end of this entry he wrote: "The wings of poets who haven't suffered barely rise from the earth. —Longfellow" (22:323–24). The apparent allusion to Longfellow stands in contrast to a concept conveyed in poem XXXV of *Versos sencillos:* "What matter, if wounds I nurse / Cloud heavens, dry seas? I maintain, / I've the sweet consolation of verse / Which rises, winged from pain."[12] The reference appears to distance Longfellow from Martí's precepts of poetry, yet in other notebook comments the Cuban called Longfellow "truly great" because he had been able to fully sense the spirit of his people while being a voice for reform in the fresh climate of a new hemisphere (21:232–33).

In his notes Martí remarked that the bard of Cambridge did not write in the midst of the forest, or in a dingy garret or warmed by the light of old books. Instead Longfellow's verses, created in an ambience of comfort, were "tranquil, bland, perfumed—as if written at an elegant table or desk" (21:232–33). This image of Longfellow stands in contrast to the setting for Poe's poem "The Raven," and suggests that Martí may have envisioned a contrast of poets in these observations.

Martí appreciated Longfellow as a professor and as a critic of literary critics. His notes include the lines "Longfellow taught the way I taught Spanish in the class on thirtieth street. Grammar through language, not language through grammar. Models and not rules" (21:406). The notebooks also contain a set of entries about literary critics, including two quotations—written in English—from Longfellow. From "Driftwood" Martí copied: "Some critics are like chimney sweepers; they put out the fire below, or frighten the swallows from their nests above; they scrape a long time in the chimney, cover themselves with soot, and bring away nothing but a bag of cinders, and then sing from the top of the house, as if they have built it" (21:421–22).[13] From chapter 13 of *Kavanagh* he included: "Critics are sentinels in the grand army of letters, stationed at the corners of newspapers and reviews, to challenge every new author" (21:421).[14]

Translations

Martí translated, in rough draft, portions of Longfellow's poetry. For "It Is Not Always May" he attempted all six stanzas but left blank spaces in some parts. He tried to keep the *a-b-a-b* rhyme of the original, and in the completed stanzas he achieved this goal, though he did not maintain the eight-syllable iambic lines. At a few points, especially in the second stanza, his translation strayed from the meaning of the original lines, but in general his version was faithful to the poem. Martí achieved a better translation in nearly sixty lines of *The Song of Hiawatha*, although some spaces were left blank and some lines were missing. Here he effectively captured the feeling of the poem, and he virtually always preserved the eight-syllable line with trochaic emphasis. Both translation drafts are collected in Martí's *Obras Completas* in volume 17 under the heading "Traducciones."

Conclusions

Longfellow was one of the first American authors to come to Martí's attention, and he remained a significant part of Martí's panorama of U.S. letters. Martí characterized Longfellow as gentle, refined, and serene and said that he created enchanting and melodic lines. Such a perspective led Martí to comment that the ability to delight a reader was an important function of poetry, and he praised Longfellow's mellifluous voice. He called Longfellow a great poet but did not rank him with Emerson and Whitman. He apparently believed that Longfellow's lack of suffering had kept him from producing the purest lyricism.

Emerson, Whitman, and Longfellow were the three major authors in Martí's review of U.S. literature. Longfellow, however, figured less prominently in Martí's chronicles than either Emerson or Whitman. Most of Martí's writing about the United States was for *La Nación*, but virtually all references to Longfellow were sent to *La Opinión Nacional*.

For readers of the Venezuelan newspaper, Martí described Longfellow's life, home, and works. He made reference to the Longfellow translations from Lope de Vega and Jorge Manrique, but without naming the works translated. He did name most of Longfellow's long works and collections, as well as a double handful of individual poems. Of these, "Excelsior" was most frequently mentioned. Martí also included in his articles brief paraphrases from "A Psalm of Life" and *Hiawatha* and alluded several times to both "The Old Clock on the Stairs" and "The Village Blacksmith" without directly naming them.

How does Longfellow fare in Martí's review of American writing? He was the subject of two brief articles published in 1882 and of occasional references, almost all in the same year. Martí undertook verse translations of two of Longfellow's poems but polished and published neither. In Martí's published work, only two paraphrases from Longfellow appear.

The fact that Martí offered only two fragments of Longfellow to his readers distinguishes the treatment of Longfellow immediately from that accorded Emerson and Whitman, from whose works Martí translated and paraphrased generously. Martí revealed a restrained enthusiasm for Longfellow, speaking of the poet chiefly in bland terms and manifesting less personal involvement than he had for Whitman and Emerson. Martí valued the consolation that a maker of tender verses could bring and appreciated that Longfellow had stirred the men, women, and children of the United States to recite poetry and reward poets. He respected Longfellow as author, critic, translator, professor of Romance literature, and language instructor, but he showed detachment in depicting a writer whose comfortable existence differed so markedly from his own.

Martí and Writers of
the Romantic Movement

Martí included many authors in his panorama of American writing but turned most frequently to those associated with Romanticism. He composed sketches of Whittier, Amos Bronson Alcott, and Louisa May Alcott and translated poetry by Poe, Whittier, and John Howard Payne. He also translated prose selections from Thoreau, Louisa May Alcott, and Lowell. To Poe, Whittier, Thoreau, the Alcotts, Irving, Bryant, Lowell, Payne, Hawthorne, and Stowe he gave attention and respect. Other authors— James Fenimore Cooper, Fitz-Greene Halleck, Paul Hamilton Hayne, and Richard Henry Stoddard—received scant review.

Several authors of the romantic period appeared in Martí's narratives in connection with public events in the 1880s. Whittier and Lowell, for example, were linked to centennial celebrations. Romantic writers, in general, were prominent at such events because as established poets they were invited to compose for and appear at the festivities. Martí commented on romantic writers in connection with a variety of circumstances and themes. Pride in seeing poets recognized and cherished in their own land prompted remarks about Whittier and Payne. Death was the occasion for Martí's essays on the Alcotts. Martí wrote of Whittier, Bryant, and Stowe in relation to the abolition movement and described the appearance of Lowell and Stoddard at the 1887 authors' reading to benefit copyright interests.

This chapter describes the ways that sixteen different writers of the romantic period figured in José Martí's works. It also shows how Martí's engagement with romantic authors affected his analysis of U.S. life and reflected his ideas about literature.

Washington Irving

Martí made early reference to America's first truly important man of letters. Writing for *La Nación* in 1883, he gave his most extensive treatment of Washington Irving, touching on the author's life, home, and works. The point of departure was a celebration of the centennial of Irving's birth—an event Martí described for readers as being tantamount to a centennial of the independence of the nation's literature. Martí explained that both Americas—his America and North America—had suffered a literary dependency on the mother countries. For Martí, Irving's discovery of literary material in the New World represented an important step in breaking such dependency (9:401–2).

In the 1883 article, Martí told of Washington Irving's comfortable background and of the congenial nature of his writing. According to Martí, Irving had experienced "sorrows the size of ants and joys as big as mountains" (9:401). His genius was like "soft moonlight," and his harmonious and cultured existence allowed words to flow from his pen "with the warm delight of love" (9:402). He was agreeable as a person and pleasing in his writing.

Martí alluded to the Irving works *Salmagundi, The Life and Voyages of Christopher Columbus,* and *Tales of the Alhambra.* He called *Salmagundi* a magazine where Irving had charmingly portrayed the New York of yesteryear. Martí believed that the work on Columbus had allowed Irving to transcend the boundaries of fatherland and fame. And, said Martí, Irving's writing about the Alhambra vividly captured the romance and ambience of the Moorish palace (9:402–3).

Martí associated Irving with both the political and the cultural independence of the United States, and he consciously linked the author who sought American themes to the patriots who sought American freedom. He recounted how the centennial of Irving's birth was celebrated at Sunnyside, the author's home, while a parallel celebration of the centenary of the disbandment of the Continental Army was held nearby. This connection allowed Martí to emphasize the importance of liberty for a writer and to remark that Washington Irving was fortunate to have been born in the fresh air of a new and free nation (9:403).

Martí's other mentions of Irving included two references to the author and two allusions to his works. In an 1884 article for *La Nación*, Martí described the English language as one in which "Irving sketched colors and Whitman created mountains of waves" (10:47). The contrast was telling and revealed the Cuban author's literary instincts: Irving produced watercolors next to Whitman's bold canvases. In another brief comment, for *El Partido Liberal* in 1889, Martí referred to Irving as the first American author of stature (12:163).

Martí wrote an article for *La Nación* in 1888 that named one of Irving's most famous characters, Rip Van Winkle. Martí told his readers that the somnolent hero's rock in the Catskills was a favorite haunt for lovers, who hoped that their happiness would last a long time, like the old man's rest (12:52). Martí also noted for *El Partido Liberal* that Irving's excellent five-volume biography of George Washington had not increased in sales despite the centennial celebration in 1889 of the first president's inauguration (13:508).[1]

William Cullen Bryant

The "pantheistic poetry of Bryant" were the words Martí used in his first written reference to William Cullen Bryant. The comment appeared in an October 1, 1881, article published in *La Opinión Nacional* (9:42). A second reference appeared shortly after in the Caracas paper when Martí named Bryant as an illustrious poet (9:73). Scarcely a month later he offered more detail about the author. For this column he wrote: "English and American critics believe that the best poetic composition published in these last years in the United States is 'The Flood of Years,' an astonishing poem by William Cullen Bryant, a poet-philosopher who paused many times in his perpetual poetical illusion to watch the centuries pass by and who surprised us and who sang of the spirit of the ages with enduring, majestic, and sober verses" (23:88).

In the following year Bryant's name continued to appear in *La Opinión Nacional*. In January Martí referred to a physical trait, the poet's "prominent forehead" (9:226). In March he alluded to Bayard Taylor's "Ode" to William Cullen Bryant, which began: "Say who shall mourn him first, / Who sang in days for Song so evil-starred."[2] Martí did not paraphrase the lines but wrote that, according to Taylor, Bryant's days were "ill-starred for poetry" (14:425). In another March entry Martí referred to Bryant as "Socratic" (13:226). In May of 1882, Martí applauded

Emerson's poem "May Day" and stated that its descriptive portions were like Bryant's translation of the *Iliad*. For Martí, however, Emerson's work was more spirited and uplifting than Bryant's (23:306).

Martí also wrote about William Cullen Bryant for *La Nación*. His May 1883 columns for the Buenos Aires paper included an assessment of a new book about the "overly agreeable" life of the American writer.[3] According to Martí, the book described William Cullen Bryant, "a white poet, in the comfortable manner of Wordsworth, not like those unfortunate and glorious poets who are nourished on their own entrails" (9:413). Although white was usually linked with high esteem in Martí's writing, here it clearly indicated blandness and mediocrity. Martí was more enthusiastic, however, in an 1884 reference, when he hailed Bryant's "majestic song" as an expression of abolitionist sentiments (10:94).

In newspaper accounts of 1888 Bryant's name appeared twice. Martí called Bryant a writer of the "Homeric era of American letters" (13:403) and alluded to the Hellenic element in his poetry (5:135). In 1889 Martí referred to Bryant in the context of a description of colleges and universities in the United States. Martí had singled out Cornell as a place that eschewed the pretension of other Ivy League schools and fostered an honest love of learning. His chronicle created an idyllic scene in which spectacled students strolled under the trees and discussed philosophy. In such a setting Martí wrote of a young man and woman carrying books, "She with a volume of Bryant and he with Walt Whitman" (12:306).

Martí's notebooks contain numerous assessments and observations about writers, and his notes indicate a lack of enthusiasm for William Cullen Bryant. Martí listed "Thanatopsis" as one of Bryant's works but said nothing about it; he referred to a biography of Bryant by Symington as "overly enthusiastic" (21:147). The notes also include in Spanish what Martí garnered from U.S. critics: "Fitzedward Hall has pointed out with harsh language the great failings in prose of the cultured Bryant, considered to be a purist, if not the greatest purist, of the American prose writers" (21:147). Another notation in Spanish read: "Bryant, in an article in the *Sun*, was judged as an artist of thought and not as a poet" (21:147).

How did Bryant rate overall? In Martí's eyes he was an important man of letters but not a great poet. Martí praised Bryant's hostility toward slavery and sympathy with the abolition movement but believed that the poet was too tepid, comfortable, and subdued to produce a truly lyrical voice. Such an evaluation underscored the Cuban patriot's preference for writers who had tasted life's bitterness and for writing that championed the oppressed.

James Fenimore Cooper

Martí's only reference to James Fenimore Cooper came in an 1881 article for *La Opinión Nacional*. In one of his commentaries about Europe, Martí recounted recent events in Italy and reported that King Humbert's queen had inquired of a wealthy American about the existence of a real literature of the United States. The American responded by sending the Italian queen a large shipment of books by U.S. authors. Among the "native" American books that delighted the queen, Martí listed a novel by Cooper, a study of the great men by Emerson, the Indian poem *Hiawatha* by Longfellow, the philosophical meditation "Thanatopsis" of Bryant, and Edgar Allan Poe's "The Raven" (14:308–9). Martí also mentioned Irving, Payne, and the historians William Hickling Prescott, George Bancroft, and John Lothrop Motley and said that a host of writers were represented in the American works received by the queen. While Martí did nothing more than include Cooper's name on a list of authors, he did so in a commentary designed to establish the worth of American literature and thereby accorded the author of *The Last of the Mohicans* a place at the table of U.S. writers.

Fitz-Greene Halleck

Fitz-Greene Halleck, like James Fenimore Cooper, was named only once in Martí's writing. In an 1888 article for *El Economista Americano*, Martí described days when William Cullen Bryant was singing to Thessaly and Halleck was celebrating Bozzaris (5:135). Martí gave only the author's last name and alluded only indirectly to the poem "Marco Bozzaris." Yet this reference to the patriotic piece, probably Halleck's most famous, is not as fleeting as it appears. "Marco Bozzaris" is one of the poems in a book titled *Patriotic Reader* that was part of Martí's personal library. Martí's copy has no notations, so we can only surmise that he read the poem.[4]

Halleck's name appeared in a Martí article about the Cuban poet José María Heredia, in a passage explaining Heredia's love of the grandiose. Martí described the era in which Heredia was born as a romantic period replete with the exploits of Bolívar, Napoleon, and Washington. As a part of this background Martí alluded to the time when "Halleck was telling of Bozzaris," a reference to Fitz-Greene Halleck's account of the death of Marco Bozzaris. Bozzaris was a chieftain in the Greek struggle for freedom begun in 1820, and his dramatic death in the storming of a Turkish camp gave his story romantic appeal.[5] Thus Martí's allusion to Halleck, while essentially designed to highlight cherished ideals, also cast favorable light on an American author.

John Howard Payne

Martí's one important reference to John Howard Payne was published in *La Nación* in May 1883. In recording recent events, Martí wrote that the city of New York was paying homage to John Payne, the poet who had died while serving as consul in Tunis and whose remains were belatedly being returned home. That a city consumed with stock market transactions would honor a poet greatly impressed Martí, and he termed the tribute "beautiful" (13:245–46).

Martí mentioned Payne's youthful venture *The Thespian Mirror* and reported on his work as an actor and dramatist. He wrote of Payne's travels, and said that in Paris the American had translated French comedies into English and had composed original works. Payne had known meager days before being named U.S. consul at Tunis, yet Martí intimated that Payne lacked the background of intensely lived experience that was necessary for a writer's maturation. Martí reported that Payne had traveled widely but, like others consumed by a desire for novelty and change, had never found "the exalted land that is one's very own" (13:246).

The most important comment on Payne came in regard to his composition *The Maid of Milan* or *Clari*. In this opera, according to Martí, Payne "sowed like tears" the verses that made him famous. Martí added: "In poetry only cries from the heart open . . . the obstinate doors of fame" (13:246). This same idea is found in the introduction to Martí's poems of exile—the lyrical expressions he called "Flowers of Exile" (16:236). In writing of Payne, Martí thus reflected his own writing and experience as well.

John Howard Payne is best known for the popular line "Be it ever so humble, there's no place like Home!" As a part of his article for *La Nación*, Martí translated this and other lines from Payne's "Home, Sweet

Home!" Martí's version took liberties with the format but gave a good rendering of Payne's immortal lines. Martí translated the first few lines of the first two stanzas and then the refrain, while in the original the refrain came only after the last two stanzas (13:246–47).[6]

The return of the author's remains to the United States some thirty years after his death elicited Martí's praise. "To know enough to honor a poet is to be one," he said. "In life the afflatus [artist's inspiration] must be there alongside the hammer. Nations must cultivate poetry as well as land" (13:247). Martí's treatment of John Howard Payne highlighted the Cuban writer's respect for a nation that could cherish its poets. Wrote Martí: "They do well to return him to his own people: the bones of poets give special virtue to the land that shelters them" (13:247).

Edgar Allan Poe

José Martí's writing on Edgar Allan Poe had two main focuses. The first was on the somber and mysterious qualities in Poe's works, and the second was on the poem "The Raven." In articles in 1887 (11:164) and 1890 (5:190) for *El Partido Liberal,* Martí made reference to the mystery of Poe's writing, and in 1885 he wrote in *La Nación* that the paintings of the Mexican artist Manuel Ocaranza were at times "symbolic and terrible like a story by Edgar Poe" (10:231).

Martí's first comment on Poe, in 1881, concerned the "The Raven" and appeared in *La Opinión Nacional.* In 1887, in his essay on Whitman, Martí wrote that "When Lilacs Last in the Dooryard Bloom'd" was "much more beautiful, strange, and profound than 'The Raven' by Poe" (13:134). And in his novel *Amistad funesta* Martí placed a volume of "The Raven" with plates by Gustave Doré in one of the scenes (18:205). In the novel he characterized Poe's raven as "frightening and fateful" and evoked the macabre flavor and mysterious nature of the Doré illustrations. He included an apparent allusion to the line in "The Raven" about "bleak December" in an 1889 article for *La Nación* (12:103), and in an 1887 letter to *El Partido Liberal* he mentioned the publication in Spanish of his friend Juan Antonio Pérez Bonalde's translation of "The Raven" (11:206).

One of Martí's most informative references to Poe was in an article titled "Critics of Chicago." In this piece he expounded on his critical stance and literary preferences and alluded to the author of "The Raven" in the process. Martí's basic premise was that rhapsody and the "sublime disorder" of inspired writing were preferable to tedium and cold logic. To underscore the point he asked: "Must we prefer Caro to Land, Gottsched to Lessing, Willis to Poe, and Laharpe to Shakespeare?" (13:462). Martí's series of contrasts put Poe opposite Nathaniel Parker Willis, a writer noted for artistic polish, and one whom Poe had praised and admired. The juxtaposition carried a note of irony, however, since the very linking that favored Poe as an author tended to discredit him as a critic.[7]

Poe appeared briefly in Martí's notes. One entry registered, in Spanish, his ability to personify: "*Poe. —Personificador de todo lo abstracto./ Gran poder para personificar*" (21:263). Then Martí entered several lines in English as quotations: "—'Sense swooning into nonsense.' / —'Fundamental basis, basis in real life, for every poem.' / —'A realm of his own imagining'" (21:263). Martí's other notebook reference to Poe commented on the poet's friend Estelle Anna Lewis, who had received undeservedly high praise from Poe; here Martí also mentioned Lewis's book of sonnets defending Poe from his detractors (21:153). Martí's notes suggest that he thought Poe's writing was removed from reality and that the author was undiscerning as a critic. Such a reading is reinforced by Martí's other comments on Poe.

Edgar Allan Poe is one of the most popular American poets in Spanish America, and numerous translations of his works, both prose and poetry, have been published. Martí was among those attempting this task, and even though his Spanish versions of "The Raven" and "Annabel Lee" are fragmentary and unfinished, they merit attention.[8]

Martí was not unaware of Spanish translations of Poe: besides the version of "The Raven" published by his friend Pérez Bonalde, Martí may have seen one by Guillermo F. Hall, which appeared in 1892 in the *Revista Ilustrada de Nueva York.*[9]

How does Martí rate as a translator of Poe's verses? Ironically, though Martí's poetic concepts were distant from Poe's, he was extremely skillful in capturing the cadence and music of the American author's lines. Pérez Bonalde's translation of "The Raven" has been considered one of the best in Spanish, yet Martí's incomplete version seems better than his friend's in several respects.[10] A comparison of the first stanzas of the two translations reveals that although Martí did not keep the rhyme at the end of the lines as Pérez Bonalde did, he maintained the internal rhyme and achieved a successful alliterative effect. Read aloud, Martí's version imparts much more of the flavor of Poe than his friend's translation.

Two recent works allow readers to see for themselves how Martí's translations of "The Raven" compare with other versions in Spanish. Leonel Antonio de la Cuesta's *Martí, traductor* (Martí as Translator) gives full-text comparisons of Poe and the Pérez Bonalde and Martí translations.[11] *El traductor Martí* (The Translator Martí) by Lourdes Arencibia Rodríguez offers line-by-line comparisons of Poe and translations by Martí, Pérez Bonalde, Rafael Lozano, and Graciela Míguez.[12]

Martí partially translated the poem "Annabel Lee" with only moderate success. Translators have struggled to capture the rhythmic and musical qualities of Poe's verse, and here Martí was no exception. But if his "Annabel Lee" failed to convey the music and cadence of the original, it did achieve rhyme, reiteration, and internal rhyme. *El traductor Martí* includes line-by-line versions of the original with translations by Martí, Fernando Maristany, and Graciela Míguez.[13]

Poe and Martí were quite dissimilar as authors and held divergent views about the function of literature. Poe promoted a dark romanticism, an aristocratic art, and a cult of art for art's sake, while Martí put his faith in poetry that was anchored in personal experience and human struggles. Poe's characters were essentially creatures of fantasy, while Martí's writing was closely tied to the drama of real life.[14] Martí did not fancy Poe or feel drawn to his gothic settings, yet he appreciated his originality. And while Martí's poetry was unlike Poe's, the Cuban was skillful in expressing lines from "The Raven" in Spanish.

Martí did not write extensively about Poe but mentioned him occasionally in articles, included references to him in the notebooks, and attempted translation of two of his poems. In this coverage, Martí sounded two primary notes: that Poe was a writer of mystery and that "The Raven" was a well-known piece. Martí accepted the need to report on Poe, but distanced himself from the author's aesthetic preferences.

Paul Hamilton Hayne

All of Martí's comments about Paul Hamilton Hayne appeared in articles written in 1881 for *La Opinión Nacional* of Venezuela. The only substantive reference was for the November "Sección Constante" column. Here

Martí claimed that Hayne was "for the impassioned Creoles of the South" like "Tennyson for the English and Longfellow for the Americans of the North" (13:69). He highlighted Hayne's regional identity and said that the writer was fifty-one years old and lived sixteen miles from a city, in a pretty little house built on top of a hill and hidden among the trees (13:69). Although Martí clearly connected Hayne to the South, he did not mention that the poet's home was near Atlanta.[15]

In an October article Martí reported that the International Exposition in Atlanta had opened with verses by Hayne, who was already celebrated as a poet (9:79). And in November Martí wrote about Hayne's "Centenary Ode."[16] Martí called the centennial poem "beautiful and spirited" and again labeled Hayne "the poet of the South" (9:91).

Richard Henry Stoddard

References to Richard Henry Stoddard were few and brief. The name appears in Martí's notes about books he planned to write and in an entry that read: "Stoddard. —Un buen poeta. 'Songs of Summer'" (21:135).

The only newspaper reference to Stoddard came in Martí's report on the 1887 authors' reading on behalf of the International Copyright League. Martí mentioned Stoddard's presence and said that the writer's gray hair looked like a turban. He did not mention that Stoddard read two of his poems at the event.[17] He did, however, write approvingly of Stoddard's role at the critic's desk of the *Mail and Express*. Martí described Stoddard as "always ready, without ceasing to write elegant satires, to recover a fallen pearl from the ground and to cast out from the garden of poetry those who did not call to him with their wings" (11:368). This characterization reflects the Cuban writer's own view that the lyric voice should rise on the wings of inspiration.

Amos Bronson Alcott

Shortly after Amos Bronson Alcott's death on March 4, 1888, Martí wrote a relatively brief article on the "Platonian," in which he emphasized the pure life of this friend of Emerson and Thoreau. Using the approach employed in the Emerson essay, Martí described Alcott before actually mentioning his name. Alcott's pure life seemed to require this respect, and throughout the article Martí praised Alcott's exemplariness, calling him an "idealist without blemish" (13:187) and writing: "His house was a cenacle; his family a garland; his existence a lily" (13:188).

Much of the article dealt with Alcott's life and his educational ventures, especially the Temple School. Martí recorded with approval Alcott's opposition to corporal punishment and rejection of rote learning for schoolchildren, and he expounded on the importance of exercising love in teaching (13:188–89). Martí also wrote of the tranquil and gentle life that Alcott spent in Concord in his later years (12:187).

Alcott was closely attuned to nature and Martí credited hard work and country living with Alcott's success in living an ideal life. Martí extolled, perhaps even envied, the calm and beauty of the rural setting where Emerson and Alcott lived. He wrote that Alcott "was not born in the city which extracts man's judgment, but in the country which orders and clarifies reason" (13:188).

Near the end of the article Martí compared Alcott to Socrates and declared that the modern-day philosopher differed in having no Xantippe. Alcott's life, according to Martí, was made pleasant by a wife who understood and encouraged his mission and was not unwilling to share his poverty. The article concluded with the words "He was a poor businessman" (13:190)—a positive rather than a negative statement, coming from Martí.

Martí associated Bronson Alcott with Emerson in several ways. He commended both men for character as well as for writing; he believed that both had benefited from living in the country, and he felt that both were fortunate in having devoted wives. Additionally, Martí saw both Alcott and Emerson as idealistic alternatives to the aggressive America of unbridled capitalist appetites.

Aside from the aforementioned article—which was not published in Martí's lifetime—Alcott appeared little in José Martí's writing. He was quoted in the essay on Emerson, and his name appeared in the notebooks. Martí's short article about Louisa May Alcott mentioned her father and said that neither of the Alcotts was known to the reading public of Spanish America (13:193). The brief tribute written in 1888, however, is Martí's chief acknowledgment of Alcott's place in American letters. There Martí listed the *Tablets*, Alcott's contributions to the *Dial*, and his

"Orphic Sayings." The major emphasis was on Alcott as an untarnished man of ideals.

Henry David Thoreau

The author of *Walden* was a subject of Martí's writing throughout the Cuban exile's life in the United States. The first reference appeared in 1881 in the "Sección Constante" of *La Opinión Nacional*. Martí gave his Caracas readers a description of Walt Whitman's visit to the gravesides of Hawthorne and Thoreau and characterized Thoreau as a "thinker, a man who lived in nature" (13:128). It was a fitting introduction to an author who was consistently identified with nature. Indeed, one of Martí's last comments, directed at those going to the country to spend time with nature, counseled taking along Thoreau as reading matter (12:434).

Among the various references to Thoreau in the *Obras Completas*, several associated him with other American writers, especially those who lived in Concord. In the articles on the Alcotts, Thoreau was depicted as a hermit and naturalist (13:187–93). In an 1882 article for *La Opinión Nacional*, Martí listed Thoreau among those associated with the Athens of the United States—Boston (9:239).

Martí also described Thoreau's writing. In an article on Henry Ward Beecher, he spoke of "Thoreau's sad and substantive expression" (13:41). In an 1889 article for *La Nación*, Martí translated a quote from a toast offered by Governor Hill of New York. The occasion was the centenary of Washington's inauguration, and the quotation from the "austere" Thoreau was part of Hill's toast to Washington: "I give you these expressive words of Thoreau: .' . . He was a proper Puritan hero. . . . He was not the darling of the people, as no man of integrity can ever be.'"[18] Martí's rendering of those lines—"Héroe puritano, que no fue en verdad el favorito de la muchedumbre, como no lo será jamás ningún hombre íntegro" (12:221)—allowed him to fully impart the flavor of Thoreau and to express qualities of American character that Martí admired.

In material for *Patria* in 1894 Martí prefaced his praise for Tomás Estrada Palma's school in upstate New York with a quotation from Thoreau's *A Week on the Concord and Merrimack Rivers*: "En verdad que no sería poca ventaja que todos los colegios estuvieran situados en la raíz de una montaña: tanta ventaja sería como una cátedra dotada con holgura. Tanta educación se saca de vivir al pie de los montes como de

vivir bajo más clásicas y pomposas alamedas" (5:435). Thoreau had written: "It would be no small advantage if every college were thus located at
the base of a mountain, as good at least as one well-endowed professor-
ship. It were as well to be educated in the shadow of a mountain as in
more classical shades."[19] Martí followed the quotation with the comment
that Thoreau was a natural man who lived frugally but absorbed knowledge liberally (5:435).

This example clearly indicates how American literature permeated
Martí's writing. The *Patria* piece was not written to let Spanish Ameri-
cans know about U.S. life; rather its function was to stir Cubans to action.
Tomás Estrada Palma was a Cuban patriot who established a school for
Latin American children in Central Valley, New York, and after Cuban
independence he became the first president of the Cuban Republic. Since
Martí had used words from Thoreau to introduce his description of
Estrada Palma's school, his article had the effect of linking a respected
American author with one of the Cuban Republic's early leaders.

Martí's most extensive treatment of Thoreau appeared in an 1887 article sent to *El Partido Liberal*. For his Mexican readers Martí wrote a
piece called "Mexico and the United States" in which he discussed
Charles Dudley Warner's travel account of Mexico. Warner had written
of Mexico's natural beauty, and Martí said that, like the Concord recluse,
Warner loved nature, though "not with the unmeasured passion of that
disconsolate hermit, but with the grace of a French artist and by virtue of
a refined and compelling need for color and beauty" (7:54). Martí continued the contrast by describing the physical features of the men. According to Martí, Thoreau was "lean, austere, with a steady sorrowful gaze,
loose and uncombed hair, smooth upper lip like a Lacedaemonian, mouth
compressed to keep in sadness, and chin tilted as if held by a chin strap"
(7:54). Martí depicted Warner as an elegant and dapper gentleman who
did not share Thoreau's serious nature.

Martí's notebooks contained several references to Thoreau. One line
read: "John Burroughs, more ingenuous, pleasant and expansive than
Thoreau" (21:282). Another entry noted that, like Emerson's, Thoreau's
essays were gathered from his journals (21:379). Martí also quoted
Thoreau describing himself as: "el transcendentalista, el místico, el filó-
sofo natural" (21: 223). The corresponding line from Thoreau's journals
was "I am a mystic, a transcendentalist, and a natural philosopher to
boot."[20]

Martí never wrote an entire article about Thoreau but did present him to readers through various quotes and comments. He did not discuss Thoreau's writing or name his works but did give a description of his physical appearance and demeanor. He placed Thoreau among the transcendentalists, linked him to other writers living in Concord, and portrayed him as a hermit, an austere man, and a lover of nature.

John Greenleaf Whittier

Martí's major piece of writing on Whittier, an 1887 sketch of three long paragraphs on the occasion of the poet's eightieth birthday, began with a description of the way the United States celebrated the birthdays of its senior poets. According to Martí, "The house is filled with flowers each new birthday; the schools declare the anniversary a holiday; the cities appoint commissions to extend their best wishes to the aged poet; the editorial houses, enriched by his verses, give some measure of their gratitude with an artistic present; the press recounts his life" (13:403). Martí offered details about the celebration at Whittier's home in Danvers, Connecticut. The octogenarian had received numerous gifts of flowers. The tents of forget-me-nots were in memory of the poems in "The Tent on the Beach," and the sprays of ferns were like those depicted in the poet's works. For a fir balsam pillow bordered with pine tassels, materials were taken from a site near Helen Hunt Jackson's grave.[21] The birthday cake bore the Whittier verse "Who loves his fellow-man wins Heaven before life closes," which Martí translated as "El que ama al hombre halla en la vida el Cielo" (13:404).[22]

Martí considered Whittier a mother-of-pearl poet. He said the Quaker poet's verses were like "the bluish haze of the hills where his home was nestled, and like the rainbow-hued pebbles the poet collected from clear streams on his long morning walks" (13:402). Yet Martí believed that Whittier's mother-of-pearl poetry had been touched with feeling and fire in *Voices of Freedom*, where the Quaker condemned "the vile slave-owners and political cowards who opposed emancipation" (13:403).

In addition, Martí mentioned the pleasingly narrated *Legends of New England* and Whittier's poetry on nature. He reported that Whittier took models from nature: for "The Tent on the Beach" a shell, for "Snow-Bound" a treetop, and for "Maud Muller" a flower and a butterfly (13:404). Martí's translation of the title "Snow-Bound" was inaccurate: he called it "Rumbo a la Nieve" (Heading for Snow), rather than suggesting a family housebound by snow. Although Martí offered only faint praise for Whittier as an author, he applauded the tributes paid to the poet and in closing his comments stated approvingly: "In such a manner does the North American celebrate his poets!" (13:404).

Martí appeared to have had readers in mind when he wrote his sketch on Whittier, but it was not published during his lifetime and thus did not reach a reading public. He did, however, inform Spanish Americans about the Quaker poet through brief references for several different newspapers.

Whittier's name appeared in various of Martí's articles about the United States. The first instance was a January 1882 "Sección Constante" column for *La Opinión Nacional*. Here Martí published his translation of some of Whittier's latest verses. His version of "Valuation"—which he did not name by title in his article—faithfully reproduced both Whittier's *a-b-a-b* rhyme and the meaning (23:143). In fact, "Valuation" is underappreciated and frequently ignored as a Martí translation. It conveyed sentiments dear to Martí—appreciation for modest income in contrast to wealth—and quite effectively reproduced Whittier's message. Only one line in the second stanza, where perhaps Martí or his typesetters strayed, is open to interpretation.[23] The verses, four stanzas of four lines each, are a dialogue between a well-to-do squire and a humble deacon in which the squire laments that heaven holds more promise for a man of modest means than for him. When the squire hints at wanting to even the score, the deacon, with a twinkle in his eye, suggests that it can easily be done if the rich man puts his coins on the same path as the deacon's. Whittier's last stanza reads:

"Well Squire," said the Deacon, with shrewd common sense,
While his eye had a twinkle of fun,
"Let your pounds take the way of my shillings and pence,
And the thing can be easily done!"[24]

The corresponding lines from Martí are:

"¡Me aflige, buen señor, de ese tesoro
Veros trémulo esclavo!
¡Ved! Echad a rodar las libras de oro
Por el camino ruin de mi centavo." (23:143)

While the poem "Valuation" has a simple theme, it holds several challenges for a translator. It is highly idiomatic and contains terms such as "deacon" for which Spanish has no ready equivalent. Martí met the challenge by conveying the dialogue with respectful forms of address and by assuming a context with terms and titles ("caballero" and "pastor") that his readers would understand.

Two other nominal references to the Quaker poet appeared in *La Opinión Nacional.* And from 1882 until 1889 Martí made comments on Whittier for *La America, El Partido Liberal,* and *La Nación.* In these references Martí characterized Whittier as a Quaker and as a vigorous opponent of slavery. In an 1887 article for *El Partido Liberal,* Martí described Whittier as "the bard who was not afraid to speak on the slave's behalf in the abolition campaign and the one they call the 'Laureate of Liberty'" (11:368). Writing for *La Nación* in 1884, Martí applauded Whittier's contribution of "Pindaric stanzas" to the abolitionists' cause (10:94), and in an 1889 letter to the Buenos Aires paper, the Cuban reporter wrote about an assembly of the Friends of the Negro to which "Whittier, the Quaker and poet of abolition, sent verses just as he had before" (11:336). Martí's allusions to Whittier also indicated the gentle and carefully crafted nature of the poet's work (11:360).

Writing on Whittier also appeared in connection with the centennial celebration of Washington's inauguration. Reporting that schoolchildren recited Whittier's poems (13:503), Martí translated the first line of the verses "From the warm palm-lands to Alaska's cold, / Repeat with us the pledge a century old!" from Whittier's "The Vow of Washington."[25] Martí's translation said simply, "desde las palmas ardientes hasta la fría Alaska" (12:219).

Martí included passing references to Whittier in his notes, but his most important comments came in newspaper articles. For these chronicles Martí emphasized Whittier's Quaker background and his opposition to slavery. Martí classified the poetry as pretty but not profound. The Cuban poet rejoiced at the honors extended to Whittier on the occasion of his eightieth birthday but did not add a personal note of praise. The interest in Whittier's poetry was sufficient for Martí to render a very fine translation of the poem "Valuation," but in general Martí considered Whittier a facile poet and his most favorable comment was about Whittier's antislavery poems.

Whittier's poem "The Worship of Nature," while not mentioned specifically by Martí, is suggestively similar in theme to the third poem of *Versos sencillos*. Whittier's poem has ten stanzas and Martí's has twelve. Both, however, have *a-b-a-b* rhyme and both proclaim that nature is a perfect setting for worship.[26] An edition of Whittier's *Complete Poetical Works* is one of the eleven books in English known to have been in Martí's personal library.[27]

Nathaniel Hawthorne

Martí expressed several key ideas about Hawthorne even though he accorded him only brief treatment, chiefly in connection with other writers. Hawthorne's name appears in Martí's articles on Whitman, Louisa May Alcott, George Bancroft, and Henry Ward Beecher. In the Alcott article Martí described Hawthorne as a "novelist of the spirit" (13:193), and in writing of Beecher, Martí made reference to the "warm, transparent, and fine prose of Nathaniel Hawthorne" (13:41). In the article on Bancroft, published in *La Nación* in 1887, Martí wrote about Hawthorne's employment in a customs position. In 1839 Bancroft, as collector at the Port of Boston, had appointed Hawthorne to a position in the Boston Custom House, and Martí explained that the eminent historian had wished in this manner to alleviate the author's poverty. Martí said that Hawthorne had complied faithfully with the requirements of the job and called this a testament to the practical ability that a "gentleman of letters" might display (13:312). Martí also described Hawthorne as an author who dug to the very bedrock of the human spirit to write *The Scarlet Letter* (13:312).

Martí's most substantive remarks about Hawthorne were published in New York in a May 1884 article for *La América*. Martí based this writing on an article called "The Salem of Hawthorne" in the *Century*, also in May 1884. The article was written by Julian Hawthorne, the author's son, and told about Hawthorne's life and work in Salem.

In writing about "The Salem of Hawthorne," Martí described the American author as a "creative, profound, and sincere novelist" who was "loved for his humility and held to be foremost among the great minds," and as a "faithful describer, a privileged observer, an artist of extreme craft, and a man imbued with subtle sensitivity to nature and her spirit"

(13:449). Martí emphasized Hawthorne's ability to capture the essence of everyday life and to depict man's spirit. According to the Cuban writer, Hawthorne had "an unusual and fortunate way of making his characters agree with the landscapes in which they moved, giving to all his novels that rich spiritual life, warm light, and perfect wholeness that makes them so worthy" (13:450). Martí seemed to paraphrase loosely Julian Hawthorne's comment in his article that Hawthorne "differs markedly from the great French novelist Balzac, who wrote by the map and the rule and always knew precisely the income of all his people and from what investments it was derived."[28] Martí rendered this idea as "Hawthorne no veía, como Balzac y los noveladores de ahora, las líneas, minuciosidades y ladrillos y tejas de los lugares que copiaba; sino su alma y lo que inspiran" (13:449–50).

Martí told how Hawthorne had written a series of fantastic stories dealing with witches and witchcraft, and he quoted Julian Hawthorne on why these tales had been burned by their author: "they embodied no moral truth; they were mere imaginative narratives, founded on history and tradition, and would not have the spiritual balance and proportion of what Hawthorne would deem a work of art."[29] Martí's account in Spanish was "no encerraban ninguna verdad moral: porque eran narraciones de pura imaginación, fundadas en la leyenda o en la historia, y no tenían aquel equilibrio y proporción espirituales que constituyen la obra de arte" (13:450).

Martí's focus on this aspect of Hawthorne's writing is significant because Martí came to similar conclusions about his own novel, *Amistad funesta*. In his prologue to what was to have been a second edition of the novel, Martí confessed his dissatisfaction: "the joys of artistic creation do not compensate for the pain of moving about in a prolonged piece of fiction, with dialogues that have never been heard, among people who have never lived" (18:192).

The *Century* magazine article on Hawthorne conveyed ideas that worked in tandem with Martí's own thoughts about literature. Martí wrote that just as blood flows beneath the surface of the skin, so must a living sentiment or a thought of permanent value lie beneath the surface in works of fantasy and imagination (13:450). Martí also expressed the idea that superior writers could not be satisfied with facile and uninspired writing. Said Martí: "To employ oneself with what is sterile when what is useful could be done; to occupy oneself with the facile when there is sufficient energy to undertake the difficult; to do this is to despoil talent of its dignity" (13:450).

Martí's comments on Hawthorne varied with the context and were often linked to other U.S. authors. His treatment of Hawthorne was largely gleaned from a magazine article written by the author's son. Much of what Martí wrote focused on Hawthorne's connections to Salem and on perspectives about literary style. Although Martí did not present Hawthorne and his works in detail, his reading of Hawthorne led to introspection and moved the Cuban to a spirited exposition of his own assumptions about literature.

James Russell Lowell

James Russell Lowell first appeared in José Martí's writings in an 1881 reference to the American author's service as ambassador to England (9:32). A year later in an article for *La Opinión Nacional*, Martí wrote that the United States had in Lowell a diplomat who because of family background, refinement, and openness of spirit was especially well suited to represent a republic in the seat of a monarchy (9:305). His assessment continued with a list of Lowell's achievements as an author: "The United States is proud of this man of letters who has written the best book in Yankee dialect, the best heroic song of the miracles and glories of the War of Independence, and the most conscientious magazine born in this nation" (9:305). The "best book in Yankee dialect" referred to *The Biglow Papers*, "the best heroic song" most likely to "Three Memorial Poems," and "the most conscientious magazine" to the *Pioneer*, a magazine begun in 1842 by Lowell and a Mr. Robert Carter.[30] Martí also mentioned Lowell's difficulties with Irish sympathizers in the United States, who believed the representative to London to be too pro-English (9:305–6). In yet another allusion to Lowell as ambassador, Martí recorded that in an unusual gesture of esteem, "the poet of the Yankee language" had been chosen rector of the University of St. Andrews (18:427).

Martí featured Lowell in his description of the 1887 reading by notable American men of letters to benefit the copyright cause. Here Martí mentioned Lowell's renown as the patriarch of genteel letters in America and his fame as the creator of the tenacious and astute Yankee sketched in *The Biglow Papers*. Martí also wrote of the "majestic" discourse on democracy that Lowell delivered in England. Lowell gave the address, said

Martí, to convince the U.S. public that he was not too pro-British (11:360–61).

In the same article Martí offered personal comments on Lowell. The author's voice was dulled with age, Martí said, and his youthful daring had surrendered to prosperity. Martí described Lowell as an author who had moved from the vigorous and challenging criticism of "A Fable for Critics" to a comfortable, conservative, and less creative stance. Martí portrayed Lowell physically as having hair parted in the middle and falling to either side, a copious beard, and long drooping mustaches. Finally, Martí said that Lowell could not be heard (11:361).

The 1889 centenary of Washington's inauguration provided another focus for Martí's treatment of Lowell. Schools were brimming with patriotism, and children learned verses such as Lowell's "Virginia gave us this imperial man" (13:503).[31] On April 30, as a part of the celebration, Lowell spoke at a banquet at the Metropolitan Opera House, where he offered a toast to literature:

> I admire our energy, our enterprise, our inventiveness, our multiplicity of resources, no man more; but it is by less visibly remunerative virtues, I persist in thinking, that nations chiefly live and feel the higher meaning of their lives. Prosperous we may be in other ways, contented with more specious successes, but the nation is a mere horde supplying figures to a census which does not acknowledge a truer prosperity and a richer contentment in the things of the mind.[32]

Martí recorded these sentiments in Spanish for the readers of an article published in June 1889 in *La Nación:*

> Admiro nuestra energía, nuestra empresa, nuestra invención fértil y nuestra abundancia de recursos; pero persisto en creer que las naciones viven principalmente por virtudes menos remunerativas. Horda es y no nación, mera horda que le da cifras al censo, aquel pueblo que no halle su principal prosperidad y su contento mejor en las cosas del espíritu. (12:222)

Martí's perfectly crafted translation of Lowell's toast is significant. It let readers in Spanish America know that authors in the United States could appreciate the intellectual and idealistic properties of literature. It established that not everyone in the colossus was mired in materialism. And it allowed Lowell's tribute to letters to be heard throughout the hemisphere. Had Rodó, the Uruguayan essayist who would later criticize the materialism of the United States, taken to heart these words by Martí, he might have been less convinced of U.S. failings in the realm of the spirit.

In January of 1890 a Martí article for *La Nación* included comment on Lowell's "iconoclastic discourse," a reference to the American author's December 1889 address to the Modern Language Association.[33] Lowell had declared the importance of modern languages in his address, and Martí alluded to those remarks as well as to Lowell's appreciation of Greek literature. The report for *La Nación* also reflected Lowell's statement, given at the Modern Language Association meeting, that "it is not the language in which a man writes but what he has been able to make that language say or sing that resists decay," sentiments Martí expressed for his readers in Spanish (13:457).[34]

Martí's notes, too, have references to Lowell and his works. Among them is the Lowell quotation "Only those languages can be called dead, in which nothing living was ever written" (22:276).[35] In another entry Martí transcribed lines from "A Fable for Critics":

He who would write and can't write can surely review.
Can set up his small booth as critic and sell us his
Petty conceit, and his pettier jealousies

and

He reviews with as much nonchalance as he whistles.—
He goes through a book and just picks out the thistles. (21:422)[36]

Another section in Martí's notes (22:51) also has lines from "A Fable for Critics." These are not identified as a quotation but are taken from Lowell's section on Holmes:

His are just the fine hands, too, to weave you a lyric
Full of fancy, firm [*sic*], feeling, or spiced with satyric
In a measure so kindly, you doubt if the toes
That are trodden upon are your own or your foes.

Martí viewed James Russell Lowell as a successful author. He remarked on his career, described his writing, discussed his public appearances, and translated his statement about "our literature." Furthermore, Martí appreciated Lowell's critical stance, especially as expressed in "A

Fable for Critics." Martí's appraisal of Lowell was positive but tempered by the author's uninspired performance at the copyright benefit.

Oliver Wendell Holmes

Martí first mentioned Oliver Wendell Holmes following the death of Longfellow. In an 1882 account sent to *La Opinión Nacional,* he wrote that the poet Holmes, along with other authors, had attended the Longfellow burial (13:230–31). Two years later Martí characterized the American author as "the album king" (8:427), presumably because Holmes wrote a poem called "Album Verses" that appeared in *The Autocrat of the Breakfast Table.* Finally, Martí's article on Whittier included Holmes as one of the "three old men"—Holmes, Whittier, and Lowell—of American literature (13:403).

Although Martí's initial references to Holmes were brief, he later became more informative. In writing of the authors' copyright reading of 1887, Martí listed Oliver Wendell Holmes as one of the writers not present. He went on to describe the Autocrat of the Breakfast Table as the writer who "in simple and sensitive prose and rhyme sang the virtues and censured the pettiness of the Bostonian" and who then "in the days of the war, coined the verses that remind one of those soldiers of Bunker Hill; with waistcoat open, hands smoking, hair disheveled, and gaze confident before the prospect of death" (11:360). Virtually the same reference appeared in an article that Martí wrote a few days later for *El Partido Liberal.* In the article for the Mexican paper, however, Martí added the description of Holmes as a "doctor-poet" (11:368)

A July 1888 article for *La Nación,* about the death of philanthropist Courtlandt Palmer, provided another reference to Holmes. Here Martí alluded to the interest Palmer took in sponsoring talks by prominent thinkers such as Emerson and Holmes (13:353). Martí's notes contain a fragment, written in English, that mentions Holmes and seems to suggest that Martí wished to attend one of the talks (22:72).

Martí's last published reference to Holmes was in 1889 in a letter for *La Opinión Pública* of Montevideo. In it Martí described the clamorous demands made by Civil War veterans and noted that neither Holmes, who was celebrating his eightieth birthday, nor his friends approved of such tactics (12:329).

Martí's correspondence also held a reference to Holmes. In a letter to

Ricardo Rodríguez Otero dated May 16, 1886, Martí outlined his ideas about Cuba and explained the folly of considering U.S. annexation of Cuba as an option. He pointed out that the United States desired Cuba only for selfish purposes and that the arrogance of the Americans' attitude was even reflected in their poetry. He sounded the warning note with a line from Holmes: "We are the Romans of the modern world,— the great assimilating people. Conflicts and conquests are of course necessary accidents with us as with our prototypes."[37] In his letter Martí rendered this as "Somos los romanos, y llegarán a ser ocupación constante nuestra la Guerra y la conquista" (1:195).

The notebooks contained passing allusions to Holmes. In one place Martí noted Holmes's latest work: "'Iron Gate'—la última obra de Holmes"; a nearby entry was simply "'Whittier-Holmes'" (21:325). There was one quotation from Holmes, in English: "The clown knows very well that the women are not in love with him, but with Hamlet, the fellow in the back [sic] coat and plumed hat. Passion never laughs" (21:418).

Oliver Wendell Holmes seems to have occupied a middle ground in Martí's scheme of U.S. authors. Martí mentioned him, gave some comment on his poetry, but never expressed a personal feeling toward him. The distinguished doctor-poet was reluctant to condemn slavery, unlike Whittier, Stowe, Bryant, and other writers, and offered no sentiments of conscience for Martí to praise. Martí's writing about Holmes was perfunctory and his appraisal of the author one of polite acceptance.

Harriet Beecher Stowe

Martí's abhorrence of slavery and his compassion for those who suffered its abuses made Harriet Beecher Stowe's landmark antislavery novel a natural subject of interest for him. As a boy in Cuba, Martí followed the events of the U.S. Civil War and very likely knew of *Uncle Tom's Cabin* even then.[38]

Martí wrote of *Uncle Tom's Cabin* in his early chronicles about the United States. In a "Sección Constante" column of 1881, he described the widespread fame of Stowe's work and reported that it was performed almost daily in some American theatre. He portrayed the author as the "fortunate novelist who sketched in clear relief, at an opportune moment, the sufferings and misery of American slaves, in a book that makes a more powerful impression because its account is neither exaggerated nor forced." In continuing his critique, Martí wrote both of Stowe and of the writer's craft in general: "Not the least of the author's merits is that she restrained her indignation and contained her anger at the same time that she detailed the torments of her characters. To do otherwise would have harmed her work. In novels, as in poetry and drama, if the writer is not a permanent and visible actor, he weakens his book and compromises its success each time that his personality manifests itself in the work." Martí also reported that *Uncle Tom's Cabin* was being sold at bargain prices in London. As an aside, he observed that the brouhaha over her "pretentious revelations"—references to Lord Byron in the book *Lady Byron Vindicated*—had not tarnished her fame (23:125–26).[39]

Subsequent references to Stowe were brief. Writing in 1882 in a column for *La Opinión Nacional*, Martí stated that critics in the United States had placed the name of novelist Frances Hodgson Burnett, author of *Little Lord Fauntleroy*, alongside that of Harriet Beecher Stowe. Martí did not comment on the merits of the linkage, so we do not know if he approved of the comparison or if he thought that Burnett's book—which launched a trend in little boys' fashions—was an appropriate companion for an antislavery novel. In his article on Henry Ward Beecher, Martí mentioned Beecher's sister Harriet as the author of *Uncle Tom's Cabin* (13:37). In an 1884 letter to *La Nación*, he described Mrs. Stowe's famous book as "the unforgettable novel that illuminated the dark heart of slavery" (10:94).

Martí repeated some of his comments about Stowe in an 1885 article for *La Nación:* her role in awakening the nation's conscience to the plight of the slave and her publication of "revelations" about Byron, which, Martí said, had not damaged her reputation. He described *Uncle Tom's Cabin* as "the voice of tears" (10:321).

In the same 1885 article and in others, Martí associated Stowe with Helen Hunt Jackson, who championed the cause of the American Indian (10:321). In an 1887 article for *La Nación* Martí again linked the two authors, suggesting that Jackson had done for the Indian what Stowe had done for the slave (11:134). In the introduction to his translation of the book *Ramona*, Martí said that Helen Hunt Jackson had written on behalf of the American Indian with more art than Harriet Beecher Stowe had employed on behalf of blacks (24:204).

Martí discussed Stowe chiefly in regard to her humanitarian values.

He made only passing reference to her in his notes and mostly brief comments in his articles. He emphasized *Uncle Tom's Cabin* and compared Stowe to Helen Hunt Jackson. Martí clearly thought that Stowe's role as an author was important and that "the voice of tears" had been of service to mankind, but he offered no new insight about either the author or her most famous work.

Louisa May Alcott

In 1888, shortly after her death, Martí wrote what are probably his only comments on Louisa May Alcott. He was interested in both the Alcotts and referred to them in his literary testament, but unfortunately neither sketch was published during his lifetime. In an article subtitled "Literary Originality in the United States," Martí presented Louisa May Alcott's life, her writing, and her literary development. By way of introduction, he criticized the stuffy world of academic writing and said that in contrast Alcott's writing was based on real-life experiences.

He gave ample treatment to her background and childhood. For example, he wrote of the privations of the Alcott home and recounted the steps in Alcott's literary career: her stories for schoolchildren, her early narratives for newspapers, her *Hospital Sketches*, and finally her well-known books such as *Little Women* and *Little Men*. Other works that Martí listed were *Work, Eight Cousins, Lulu's Library, Under the Lilacs*, "Bertha," and "The Rival Prima Donnas." Martí said that much of the author's life was depicted in *Work* and *Little Women*.

Martí's article also included two lengthy quotations from Alcott's *Hospital Sketches*. He believed that the empathy evoked by these experiences had helped Alcott find her best expression as an author and reported that after *Hospital Sketches* "she wrote nothing but the truth" (13:194). Martí offered Spanish versions of two selections from *Hospital Sketches*, actually improving upon them in translation. The first quotation described the disheveled appearance and disheartened state of Union soldiers following the rout at Fredericksburg. The second related what happened when Alcott offered food to one of the soldiers.[40]

Qualities in Louisa May Alcott's writing that attracted Martí were proportion, naturalness, and good taste (13:194). He also applauded the veracity of her characters, citing as examples "tom-boy Jo" and "good-natured Christie." Of her works, especially *Little Men* and *Little Women*,

Martí remarked: "There life sparkles, without vain images or severe descriptions; virtue enters the soul as you read, like balm dressing a wound" (13:195).

Like her father, Amos Bronson Alcott, Louisa May was associated in Martí's writing with the Boston-Concord group of writers whom Martí particularly admired. He said that Louisa May Alcott spent childhood years living not far from such writers as Thoreau, Hawthorne, and Emerson and that a commendable characteristic held in common by all of those writers was a love for mankind as well as a love of letters (13:195). Martí lamented that Louisa May Alcott was not known in Spanish America, just as her father the philosopher was not known (13:193). His statement points to his concern about informing the citizens of his America about the writers and writing of the United States, and it is unfortunate that his comments on and translations of the author of *Little Women* did not reach a Spanish-speaking public during his lifetime. Nonetheless, more than a century later, Martí's sketch of Louisa May Alcott is still an excellent introduction to one of North America's most popular female authors.

Martí and Writers of Realism

After the Civil War, America's focus moved west. In a sense, Martí's depiction of American writing moved west also, as he dealt with the realistic novel, frontier tales, balladeers, and Indian lore. Toward the end of Martí's residence in the United States, his comment on American authors reflected the shifting national panorama. In the late 1880s, writers of the Northeast and South continued as a presence in his work, but he wrote increasingly of authors whose works were set in Indiana, Missouri, California, or the western territories. Martí's writing about literature of the postromantic era was marked by a preoccupation with issues of justice, American expansionism, and questions of sacrifice.

Martí wrote less about American writers of the period of realism than he did about romantic writers. Nonetheless, he commented extensively on Mark Twain, referred frequently to William Dean Howells, and took considerable interest in Helen Hunt Jackson and her works. He gave only fleeting attention to humorists and local color writers. He mentioned Henry Wheeler Shaw and David Ross Locke among the humorists and wrote of George Washington Cable, James Whitcomb Riley, Joaquin Miller, John Hay, Bret Harte, Edward Eggleston, and Will Carleton as depictors of local scenery. Finally, Martí discussed or noted in brief fashion a diverse array of other authors: Frank R. Stockton, Sidney Lanier, Edward Everett Hale, Edward Bellamy, Henry James, George William Curtis, Charles Dudley Warner, and John Burroughs.

Martí's interest in Mark Twain and Helen Hunt Jackson sprang mainly from the social messages he found in their texts. Howells appeared with some frequency because of his prominence in the press. As humor, local color, and dialect had little appeal for Martí, the writers of these genres got scant attention in his chronicles. Martí's connection with and reaction to the remaining authors cannot be easily categorized. Some he treated with stock description; others evoked respect (Curtis) or a mixture of interest and indignation (Warner).

Not a single author in the realist group was featured by Martí in an essay or literary sketch, and only Helen Hunt Jackson attracted his sustained interest as a translator. Instead, he reported on most of these writers in comments interspersed with items of current news. Martí mentioned many of them either at the time of their death or in connection with a lecture or special event. He wrote of Lanier, Shaw, and Locke only after they had died, and remarked upon Riley, Cable, Miller, Harte, Hay, Eggleston, Carleton, Stockton, Twain, and Howells in relation to public appearances. Martí wrote of Twain and Cable on their lecture tour during the winter of 1884–85 and included Riley, Twain, Cable, Miller, Harte, Hay, Eggleston, Carleton, Stockton, Howells, Warner, and Curtis in comments about an authors' reading on behalf of copyright protection held at Chickering Hall in November of 1887.

Unpublished material constituted a considerable portion of Martí's assessment of late nineteenth-century writers. Many of his most important comments about authors of the realist period appeared not in articles but in notes and correspondence. This is especially true for Helen Hunt Jackson and Mark Twain, but also for Joaquin Miller, John Hay, Henry James, and Charles Dudley Warner. With the exceptions of Jackson and Twain, Martí's writing did not have a major impact in introducing these authors to Latin American readers. His comments on realist writers did, however, continue to form part of his panorama of U.S. life and to elicit Martí's personal perspectives about the purpose and properties of literature.

Mark Twain

Martí's first reference to Mark Twain, written in somewhat stilted English, appeared in 1880 in one of his "Impressions of America by a very fresh Spaniard" for the *Hour*. In this article Martí reported: "There is among the Americans, the humorist Mark Twain—and has he not presented the gifted king of Bavaria, a poet, an enthusiast, a knight of old times, as a savage who obliged the singers of his theatre to play the same opera twice in a night, under the most terrible rain that could fall over the

poor Bavarians? He astonishes himself with the mastodontic composition of German words" (19:122). What was Martí trying to describe? His
reference was to an incident portrayed in Twain's *A Tramp Abroad*. The
Bavarian king had required an entire opera company to repeat a performance just for him and demanded that the stage manager douse the ac-
tors with "rain" from the overhead water pipes to make the storm scenes
seem real.[1] Martí's early comments on Mark Twain were marred by the
limitations of his English and thus failed to capture the flavor of the
American author's travel literature. His later references, written in Spanish, provided far more effective portraits.

Nearly five years passed before Martí renewed his interest in Mark
Twain. The occasion was a New York appearance by Twain and George W.
Cable on the lecture circuit, which Martí described for readers of *La
Nación*. Twain and Cable, he wrote, were authors who drew their literary
inspiration from life rather than books (10:131–32). He reinforced this
precept with a statement that reflected his own thinking: "A living, bleed-
ing soul must be palpable beneath the surface of writing" (10:132). Martí
had expressed the same sentiment in writing about Nathaniel Hawthorne in May of 1884, and it set the tone for much of his commentary on
Mark Twain.

Comments on the man who took his nom de plume from the Mississippi River accounted for almost a third of Martí's article. He explained
that Samuel Clemens's pen name was the boatman's cry "mark twain,"
and he gave the Spanish equivalent, "en dos brazas," to make the meaning clear to his readers. Martí pointed out that the American writer's
originality extended to his choice of a name.

Martí considered originality and freshness the hallmarks of Mark
Twain's writing. Although he did not hail the American humorist as a
great literary light, he appreciated the fact that Twain's light was very
much his own—a quality that had rightfully earned him fame in both
Europe and the United States.

Interspersed with remarks about the author and his works, Martí's
own perspective on literature was revealed. The Cuban inveighed against
overwrought writing and belittled coquettish literature created principally for display. In letters, he insisted, "one needed to be a missionary,
not a narcissist" (10:134–35). He criticized the authors of the day for being "gilders" who fancied form and ornament, and said that literature

needed miners—men whose aching hands dug deep to bring forth the purest ore (10:135). Martí clearly meant these remarks to be favorable to Mark Twain, whom he considered one of the "miners."

Martí viewed Twain's variety of experiences and his travel vignettes with appreciation because they imbued the American's writing with the colors of real life and allowed him to observe mankind's foibles in various locales. Martí reported that Twain had lived in the midst of the forging of a frontier, that he knew men well enough to see through disguise and façade, and that he showed them as they really were (10:135–36). In describing the writer's technique, Martí said: "He sketches in charcoal but with sure and swift lines. He understands the power of adjectives, the adjectives that economize sentences, and he heaps them upon a character in such a way that the man described gets up and walks like a live man" (10:136). According to Martí, the American author was able to depict with skill because he observed with skill. Twain's vision was grounded in reality because he had experienced much and understood suffering (10:136). For Martí the only drawback to such a grounded approach was that it might keep an author from appreciating the idealistic horizons (10:137). Twain's novels, wrote Martí, lacked cohesion (10:137).

Buenos Aires readers learned from Martí that Twain was known in Europe and that *Le Figaro* of Paris had translated and praised his works. Such popularity was not due to a polished style but rather to the American author's subtleties of observation. Twain knew his audience, Martí said, and understood that the public did not look to him for refinement (10:137).

Martí included information about Twain's life and works: the author's marriage to a rich woman, his travels to the Sandwich Islands, Europe, Egypt, and Palestine, and the fame and monetary success of his travel books (10:136). To shed light on the reasons for this success, Martí described an episode from *The Innocents Abroad* in which Twain makes a bet with an Arab at the pyramids in Egypt.[2] While Martí did not attempt to translate the vignette, he presented it in such a way that even those who knew little about Mark Twain could taste the flavor of the travelogue (10:136–37). Martí listed as specific works *The Innocents Abroad*, *A Tramp Abroad*, and a work he called "Los Inocentes en Casa," which was likely a reference to *Roughing It*, Twain's travel narrative of the American West (10:137).

No report about the famous American humorist would be complete without a comment on humor, and Martí's critique said of Twain: "He writes books swollen with satire, to make one laugh, and the humor comes not from presenting ludicrous or exaggerated figures but from portraying in clear relief, and with an air of picaresque innocence, the contradictions, failings, and hypocrisies of everyday people. He manages to contrast exceedingly well what people affect that they think and feel and what they really think and feel" (10:134). Martí felt that Twain accomplished all of this in such a way that people could laugh at themselves, and he characterized Twain's brand of humor as having the rough-hewn stamp of the author's own life (10:136).

As a writer who excelled as an orator and public speaker, Martí was willing to critique Twain and others who spoke and read in public. He reported that Twain had the habit of winking, perhaps to see better or perhaps to keep others from reading his thoughts (20:135). And he remarked on the comic effect produced by the author's nasal tone and style of delivery (10:137). Of Twain as a speaker, Martí gave this account: "He recites, hurriedly and as if he didn't want to, incidents from his life and works: he comes onstage haltingly and seems bored: he reads his story to the public as he might read to his children, in order to entertain them and then be rid of them" (10:137).

In describing Twain's appearance, Martí was more benign. "He has a white shock of hair: his eyes bespeak experience, profundity, and roguishness: the nose long and aquiline dominates a martial mustache: the rest of the face, of healthy color, is smooth shaven: he throws his head forward like one who scrutinizes: and his shoulders are held high as if he had decided to shrug his shoulders forever" (10:137). Such was the portrait of the man Martí called "the foremost American humorist" (10:135).

In a March 1886 article for *La Nación*, Martí referred to Mark Twain as a strong supporter of copyright protection for writers (10:388). Twain was also one of the authors at the 1887 Copyright League gathering, and Martí wrote for *La Nación* of Twain's literary originality, his free and tumultuous life, and his fame on both sides of the Atlantic. The selection of an original and authentic pen name revealed for Martí how the writer of frontier humor had taken his material from the very heart of experience (11:360). A letter just a few days later for *El Partido Liberal* very nearly duplicated the comments in *La Nación* and added a note about Twain's satirical humor (11:368).

Martí's major engagement with Twain became manifest in his report-age and correspondence of 1890 and was inspired by interest in *A Connecticut Yankee in King Arthur's Court*. Writing for *La Nación* in January of 1890, Martí included a lengthy comment about the author's home in Hartford, *Roughing It, The Innocents Abroad, A Tramp Abroad,* and *A Connecticut Yankee*. He described these books as the products of a mature writer, and felt the last to be the culminating piece (13:459). Martí saw in the work an American author's exasperation over injustice and a reflection of the climate of complicity and exploitation in the United States (13:459–60).

Martí compared *A Connecticut Yankee* to *Don Quixote* and claimed they belonged side by side in libraries. For Martí the *Quixote* revealed more of the sadness and truth of man's experience, while the *Yankee* burst forth with greater indignation (13:460). Martí gave his readers a summary of the plot, something he did not do for other works of fiction by American writers, and commented enthusiastically on several of the episodes. The scene where the Yankee, armed only with a lariat and a revolver, sets out to do battle with Sir Sagramor and the one where the Yankee and his fifty-two men conquer an army of twenty-five thousand knights elicited exclamations of praise from Martí. Either Martí or his typesetters mistakenly put "Lagramor" for Sagramor and gave the protagonist's name as "Jin," but overall Martí's chronicle gave an accurate summary of the work (13:460).[3]

The vocabulary of the novel, according to Martí, included both Yankeeisms and the chivalric parlance of old. Of style he remarked that Twain preferred words pared to the bone to words clothed with ideas. Another line stated one of Martí's basic tenets: "The language is of course literary since it is energetic and natural" (13:460). For Martí the fact that the author appeared from time to time in the work did not detract from its appeal. Further, Martí asserted that the work was useful because, although said to be humorous, it had been written in the wake of tears (13:461).

In writing of *A Connecticut Yankee* Martí displayed a degree of involvement and appreciation reserved for writers and works that he truly admired. He felt empathy for the strong humanitarian undercurrent of the work. His article for the Argentine newspaper stated: "There are paragraphs in Mark Twain's book that make one want to set out for Hartford to shake his hand" (13:460). Martí's one other reference to Twain for

La Nación was written just days before the extended comment of 1890. Here Martí alluded to *A Connecticut Yankee* indirectly, comparing the injustices painted in Mark Twain's medieval baronies to the abuses perpetrated by robber barons of the Gilded Age (12:337).

The most telling remarks about *A Connecticut Yankee* appeared in Martí's correspondence. A letter of April 1889 written to his close friend Manuel Mercado said that he had a new book for Mercado's son, *The Yankee* by Mark Twain (20:144). And a letter written January 2, 1890, to Gonzalo de Quesada expressed poignant appreciation for Twain's work: "Have you read the latest book by Mark Twain? I never wanted to read him much because from what I knew of him I learned nothing and his jokes were of the coarse frontier type. But this *Yankee in King Arthur's Court* is a service to humanity, with light and distinctive language and a deep and meaningful message." Martí mentioned the Yankee's defeat of twenty-five thousand fully armed knights and said: "that's why I am telling you about this book." Finally he proclaimed: "It is a book of humor that calls forth tears" (20:363).

Martí's notes contain a few brief references to Mark Twain. In one place the Cuban author entered: "Mark Twain—humorista americano, descriptor del oeste.—Autor del *Mighty Dollar* (teatro).—*Tramp through Europe.*—Col. Dick and Col. Jack—" (21:231). Other notebook references concerned the success of *The Innocents Abroad.* Martí noted that this book, which ultimately brought the publishers seventy-five thousand dollars, was reluctantly considered at first (21:397). Another notation read in English: "*Innocents Abroad* was black with handling before it was put into print" (21:420).

The author who took his name from the Mississippi River and his books from experience and observation warranted Martí's attention over a generous span of years—1880–90. Martí's appreciation for Twain grew over this decade, and the discovery of *A Connecticut Yankee,* published in 1889, sparked a reassessment of Twain's merit. Martí's writing about Mark Twain included both factual information and expressions of personal opinion. He gave readers a thumbnail sketch of *A Connecticut Yankee,* described several of its episodes, and offered his interpretation of the book. He also described a passage from *A Tramp Abroad* and one from *The Innocents Abroad.* Finally he made passing reference to the author's life and critiqued his public appearance.

The Yankee machinist's triumphs in King Arthur's England and his success against vain knighthood reached Martí *as reader* at the very time he was beginning in earnest his campaign for a new Cuban struggle. Martí saw in Twain's work a cry against injustice, a challenge to hypocrisy, and an exposé of the abuses of power and wealth. He saw direct application of its message to his own day and age and gave the book an optimistic interpretation that reflected his own hopes for the future. As a prominent critic has noted, "His interest in the fight of the few against the powerful many reveals the hand of the revolutionary faced with the overwhelming odds of the Spanish forces in Cuba."[4] Martí's analysis of the *Yankee* also touched on the kinship of Twain's work to the *Quixote,* and he recognized the relationship at a time when many American critics—William Dean Howells was an exception—were content to compare Twain's novel to Sir Thomas Malory's *Morte d'Arthur.*[5]

Martí's approach to Mark Twain had various facets. Martí did not regard him as a major writer but praised his originality and powers of description. He credited Twain with having experienced life fully and having undergone suffering, two factors that Martí deemed important for the development of mature writing. Martí was disinclined to like Twain the humorist and the nasal-pitched lecturer but was deeply moved by Twain the champion of social conscience and reform. Finally, Martí helped to introduce this author to Spanish American readers. Prior to the articles for *La Nación* little had been written in Spanish about the man Martí called America's foremost humorist.[6]

William Dean Howells

Martí's earliest comment on Howells appeared for the Venezuelan paper *La Opinión Nacional* in 1882, identifying him as one of the authors attending Longfellow's funeral (13:230). Several years later, Martí referred to Howells as a novelist from Massachusetts whose fame was just beginning (8:427).

Reaction to the Chicago Haymarket riot of 1886 produced one of Martí's most sympathetic depictions of Howells. In a letter for *La Nación* dated November 1887, Martí described the national climate surrounding the trial of the anarchists. Most of the American public was unsympathetic to the anarchists, but the "Bostonian novelist" urged clemency for the men on trial. Martí characterized Howells's stance, which had cost the author both fame and friendships, as "generous" (11:334).[7]

In December 1887 when Martí wrote for *La Nación* and *El Partido Liberal* about the reading on behalf of the International Copyright League, he mentioned Howells as one of the authors present for the event (11:360, 369). For his Mexican readership Martí added that Howells was greeted by vigorous applause from the audience (11:370). For both papers Martí reported that Howells earned more than ten thousand dollars a year but said that his novels had stooped to the commonplace of realism not because the author lacked talent but because the lives of the people he described were mundane. Martí criticized the lack of creativity of this "false literary code" and added a final reproach: "Reproducing is not the same as creating, and man's obligation is to create" (11:361, 370).

Martí made several references to the American novelist in 1889 and 1890. An article in *La Nación* described the Howells novel *A Chance Acquaintance* as a love story replete with class struggle and imbued with the romance and adventure of its Canadian setting. Martí also highlighted the novel's depiction of Canadian cities and scenery (12:113). A subsequent letter for the Buenos Aires newspaper reported Howells's annoyance over U.S. interests in Samoa and called Howells the subtle novelist who "portrayed equally well the love of a poor Italian priest and the mental ruses of a Boston pettifogger" (12:239).

In December 1889 Martí wrote about President Harrison's message to Congress and the president's expressed desire to be hospitable to immigrants while screening for those likely to oppose the social order or challenge the nation's laws. Within this context Martí reported that challenges to American society seemed threatening when heard from an immigrant voice but were acceptable if expressed by someone like Howells (12:365). In August 1890 Martí wrote that Howells's latest novel, *The Shadow of a Dream*, made good reading for those heading to the country. He described the novel's message, gently conveyed, as the folly of a married couple having a friend share their home (12:434).

In 1892 Martí included a comment in *Patria* about Luis Baralt, whose home was a prime gathering spot for New Yorkers and who had been called an "admirable man" by Howells (5:356). Martí's notebooks also included references to Howells. One read simply: "Notas del 'Pordenone' de W. D. Howells" and was followed by a number of entries in English (21:351). The title refers to a Howells poem about the Venetian fresco painter Pordenone, and the sections in English are lines from various parts of this poem.[8] Another note alluded to an article by Howells for the

August 1890 *Harper's* (21:422). The article was actually a column called "Editor's Study" that Howells wrote for the magazine, and his August 1890 topic was literary criticism by anonymous reviewers. Quite likely Martí noted the column because he shared Howells's opinion that a critic who wrote—either favorably or unfavorably—about an author's work should at least be willing to sign his name to the review.[9]

William Dean Howells shared Martí's empathy for the downtrodden characters in Mark Twain's *A Connecticut Yankee* and interpreted the novel's importance much as Martí did, but nothing indicates that the Cuban writer was aware of this convergence of interest and critique.[10] Aware or not, Martí had a matter-of-fact approach to Howells and his works. He wrote virtually nothing about the author's life and referred to his novels and criticism only in passing. Martí as Cuban patriot, concerned over U.S. expansionism and conscious of persistent problems in the American social order, noted with seeming approval Howells's attitude about these issues. In no way, however, did he register any sort of sympathy for Howells. Despite a shared social outlook, Martí's comments on the Dean of American Letters were perfunctory and lukewarm.

Helen Hunt Jackson

Helen Hunt Jackson occupied a unique place in Martí's consideration of American authors. In 1888 Martí published his translation of Jackson's *Ramona* and did so as a self-financed undertaking. His enthusiasm for Jackson is evident from his introduction to the *Ramona* translation, where he claimed: "This book is real but it is beautiful. The words sparkle like jewels" (24:203). In a letter to Manuel Mercado, Martí said of *Ramona*: "I chose it, I want you to know, because it is a book about Mexico written by an American woman with a very noble heart" (20:112–13). Martí's letters to Manuel Mercado further reveal that he had a compelling interest in seeing the translation succeed financially in Mexico and that he concerned himself with the details of distribution and sales (20:112–46).

Martí had multiple reasons for making a translation of *Ramona* available in Spanish. Both the theme and the style pleased him. He felt drawn to its message about the Indians in California under Anglo domination and took great pains over the book's sale in Mexico because he believed it would warn Mexicans of the perils of American control: "I have read few [books] of its type where nature is painted with more art, and an original land so clearly seen by a foreigner, and our people—so often disdained without reason—treated with open affection and recognition of their worth. And all this by a famous writer from the ranks of those who disdain us" (20:113).

In Martí's introduction to the translation of *Ramona*, he praised the author and her novel. The characters lingered in a reader's memory, he said, and one felt almost obliged to thank the author and go shake her hand (24:204). Martí believed the book would reach virtually all readers because it offered "merit for the literary man, color for the artist, encouragement for the noble, a lesson for politicians, an example for lovers, and entertainment for the weary" (24:205). Martí's introduction also mentioned Jackson's book *A Century of Dishonor*, spoke of her poetry, and alluded to her friendship with Emerson (24:204).

Martí's Spanish version of *Ramona* is shorter than the original and is considered by many who have compared the texts to be an improvement.[11] Essentially Martí kept the action and characters intact but abbreviated descriptions and reduced some dialogue. He gave titles to each chapter although in the original they were simply numbered. His choice of names was particularly felicitous. Alessandro took on a more virile cast as Alejandro; Father Salvierderra, the good priest, became Padre Salvatierra—literally the "landsaving" priest. Martí's translation made no attempt to imitate the highly colloquial Tennessee language of the Hyer family, and in that sense lacked the linguistic variety and unique Americana stamp of Jackson's *Ramona*. The work stands, nonetheless, as an excellent literary translation, its success all the more remarkable since Martí undertook the task in the midst of a hectic schedule of work and obligations. His secretary/assistant, Felix Sánchez Iznaga, described Martí as dictating the work at an almost feverish pace as he strode through the office with English text in hand.[12]

Martí had other connections to Jackson besides his translation of *Ramona*. An 1887 article for *El Partido Liberal* mentioned a pilgrimage made by friends to the grave of the author of *Ramona* (7:51). The same piece reviewed Charles Dudley Warner's travel narrative on Mexico and chastised Warner for writing about the lack of progress by Indians in Mexico while ignoring the misery in his own backyard. Martí continued: Had Helen Hunt Jackson not characterized U.S. Indian policy as a "century of dishonor"? (7:54–56). Martí also invoked Jackson's name in his article on Whittier, reporting that one of the gifts for the poet's eightieth birthday was a fir balsam pillow with pine tassels gathered at Helen Hunt Jackson's grave (13:404).

Martí also linked Jackson to Harriet Beecher Stowe because he saw the two authors as voices of social conscience for the United States. In his introduction to *Ramona*, Martí called Jackson's work another *Uncle Tom's Cabin* without the weaknesses of Harriet Beecher Stowe's novel (24:204). In 1885 he let readers of *La Nación* know that Stowe had decried the evils of slavery just as another woman had toiled through the years to alleviate the misery of American Indians (10:321). Martí also noted that Helen Hunt Jackson had written a deathbed letter thanking President Cleveland for his recognition of the Indian right to justice and human dignity (10:321–22). Later Martí again linked *Uncle Tom's Cabin* and *Ramona* and described the latter as an enchanting book about California life that dealt with the clash of cultures and the alliance between the upper class and the Church. Martí also characterized the work as an elegy for Indians (11:134). His account said that the author of *Ramona* lay buried on a hill in a region where she had seen Indians suffer much, that Indians—aware of her efforts on their behalf—brought offerings and flowers to her burial place, and that a newly founded school for Indians bore the name Ramona (11:134).

Martí also appreciated Jackson's poetry. In a brief piece written in 1889 for *La Juventud,* he gave the first four lines—which are also the last four lines—of her poem "The Way to Sing" (5:160–61). In writing of José Joaquín Palma, a Cuban poet visiting New York on his way to Guatemala, Martí declared that one could say of Palma and his engaging poetry what Helen Hunt Jackson had said in her "diamond-chiseled" verses: "The birds must know. Who wisely sings / Will sing as they; / The common air has generous wings / Songs make their way."[13] Martí's version of these lines was "Las aves deben saber; el que cante con juicio, cantará como las aves; el aire libre tiene alas generosas; los cantos hacen su camino" (5:161).

Martí also wrote a Jackson-inspired poem for his magazine for children, *La Edad de Oro*. Martí gave this adaptation of Jackson's "The Prince Is Dead" the title "Los dos príncipes" (The Two Princes) and noted that it was based on an idea from the American poet (18:372). In Jackson's poem the death of a king's son is contrasted with the death of a peasant boy, and each of the two stanzas concludes with the line "The Prince is dead."[14]

Martí's version conveyed the concept that rich and poor are alike in facing the death of a son and that the poor lad is no less a prince than the royal one, but Martí made the point by speaking of two princes rather than one (18:372).

Two other thematically linked poems accompanied Martí's adaptation of "The Prince Is Dead" in *La Edad de Oro*: his translation of the Emerson poem "Fable" and his own "Los zapaticos de rosa" (The Rose-Colored Slippers). In Emerson's work a squirrel explains to a mountain that each of them—one large and magnificent, one small and agile—has a purpose and that each one is worthy in its own way. In "Los zapaticos de rosa" a rich girl, Pilar, shares her rose-colored slippers with a poor child who is barefoot—underscoring the idea that each child is deserving and each one worthy in her own way.

These three works—the Emerson translation and "Los zapaticos de rosa" and the stanzas based on the Helen Hunt Jackson poem—all gave moral examples to the readers of *La Edad de Oro*. Martí's presentation also highlighted American authors he respected, and connected their work to his. The three poems created a progression of sentiments that linked Emerson to Jackson and both American authors to Martí. Taken together, the poems formed a laurel of "good works"—with Helen Hunt Jackson at the center.[15]

Notebook references provide further evidence of Martí's interest in Jackson. Some lines appear to be drafts for his translation of *Ramona* (22:66), and others suggest his awareness of reviews of the book (22:178). An entry in English appears designed to accompany a copy of the book to a bookseller: "I hope that *Ramona*, in this translation in which I have put all my heart, may be considered by you as the occasion of a not unprofitable or disagreeable acquaintance" (22:288).

Martí's writing about Jackson focused on important facets of her life and works. He twice made reference to *A Century of Dishonor*, Jackson's account of the shameful treatment of Indians in the United States.[16] He alluded to her friendship with Emerson. And he noted that her deathbed letter to President Cleveland thanked him for his concern for Indians' rights. Jackson, in fact, had sent *A Century of Dishonor* at her own expense to every member of Congress, was known for the fact that Emerson carried her odes in his pocket, and is frequently mentioned for her deathbed message to Grover Cleveland.[17]

Helen Hunt Jackson fares less well among critics and scholars today than she did among her contemporaries; nonetheless she is an author whose work has endured. She was greatly admired by both Emerson and Emily Dickinson. *Ramona* has never been out of print and survives not only as a novel but also in film, radio-theatre drama, and song.[18] A Ramona Pageant based on Jackson's work began in 1923 in southern California and has been one of the state's most spectacular outdoor events, even featuring Raquel Welch in the role of Ramona.[19]

David Ross Locke (Petroleum V. Nasby)

Martí's only references to Locke came at the time of the latter's death. Martí wrote of the passing of Petroleum Nasby, "the satirist of the war," in a February 1888 article for *La Nación* (11:409). A longer comment appeared at the beginning of the unpublished article on Amos Bronson Alcott. "The satirist David Locke, celebrated under his pseudonym of 'Petroleum V. Nasby,'" Martí observed there, was among the famous men who had recently died (13:187). Martí wrote that Locke had "contributed to the triumph of the war against the South and to the benevolence of the victors, with his critical letters which delighted Lincoln." Saying that the letters' exaggerated humor proved a useful vehicle for just ideas, Martí compared Nasby's comic approach to that of a medieval jester whose buffoonery allowed him to be a spokesman for liberty (13:187). Martí's appreciation of Locke's humor recalls the sarcastic dialogue of *El Diablo Cojuelo*, the one-issue patriotic journal he published as a boy in Cuba (1:31–36). It also calls to mind his review of the paintings of Eduardo Zamacois, written in English for the *Hour*. Martí praised the Spanish painter's portrayal of abuses and hypocrisies and stated that the "mimicry of individuals and the exaggeration of human foibles, however contemptible it may seem to great hearts, is useful and salutary" (28:134).

Henry Wheeler Shaw (Josh Billings)

Henry Wheeler Shaw's name appeared only once in Martí's writing. In an 1885 article for *La Nación*, he recorded the death of "'Josh Billings,' who wrote with great success in burlesque Yankee style" (10:227).

George Washington Cable

Cable's light flickered only briefly in Martí's review of U.S. authors. Martí's first reference was for *La Nación*, the second for *El Partido Liberal*. When Twain and Cable appeared together in New York at a lecture/ recitation in 1884, Martí described them as two of the most famous writers of the United States and as men who took literature from nature, not from libraries (10:132). He called Cable "the sagacious novelist of the South" and compared him to the Spanish novelist Benito Pérez Galdós (10:132). According to Martí, Cable was a "Pérez Galdós from New Orleans" who was precise, industrious, and touching, like the Spanish writer (10:132). Cable appeared again in Martí's reports as an author at the copyright benefit in 1887. Here Martí identified Cable as the writer whose novels painted the complexities and contradictions of southern Creole life (11:369). Cable's stage presence found favor with Martí who said that, except for Twain, Cable, and Riley, the authors seemed like schoolboys stepping up to receive a prize (11:370). Martí's overall assessment of Cable was sympathetic. He identified him as a portrayer of the Creole South, but said little about the author's style and listed none of his works.

James Whitcomb Riley

The Hoosier poet seems an unlikely candidate for words of praise from Martí, yet he fared well in Martí's accounts. After the 1887 copyright reading in New York, Martí described him as the writer "who seemed the best of them all, because he makes you laugh, and with his nose alone, which is grumbling and opulent, he tells stories" (11:360). Newspaper reports of the "reading" confirm that Riley's recitation was a huge success and that he was very well received by the audience.[20] In his articles for *El Partido Liberal* and *La Nación*, Martí called Riley the poet of the West who was said to deserve fame not yet attained (11:360). Riley was able to sketch an Indiana or Missouri man complete with bushy mustache and boots in just three or four strokes of precise verse (11:360). Martí compared this to the way a Chinese artist, with a few deft turns of his palette knife, could create a cast of characters (11:360).

Joaquin Miller

Like many other authors, Joaquin Miller appeared in Martí's writing about the International Copyright Benefit of 1887. Martí listed Miller as one of the authors not present and described him as the "poet of the Sierra" (11:360–68), a nod to Miller's book of poems *Songs of the Sierras.*

Martí's main focus on Joaquin Miller, however, concerned his empathy for Native Americans. In his notes Martí made two references to Miller's concern for the American Indian: a reminder to purchase *My Own Story* and a passage from it where Miller said that he owed the white man nothing and the Indian much in terms of life's values (21:420–21).

John Hay

In a December 1886 letter for *La Nación* Martí noted "a new history of Abraham Lincoln, written by his secretaries L. Nichols and Hay" (13:155). In this manner he introduced the name of American author John Hay, who had served on Lincoln's staff. Martí added that this was a "sincere, sound, and powerful book" (13:155). Hay was also among the writers Martí discussed in articles about the International Copyright Benefit of 1887. Martí's articles sent to *La Nación* and *El Partido Liberal* characterized Hay as an author who described the deeds, romance, and adventures of the American West with the language and flavor of the region (11:368).

A more compelling reference to John Hay is an entry in Martí's notes under the heading "English and U.S. poems I should remember": "'Jim Bludso,' written in the dialect of the West by John Hay" (22:276). The short ballad "Jim Bludso" tells in folksy language the story of a steamboat engineer—no stranger to sin—who sacrifices his life to keep others from perishing. After fire breaks out, the engineer stays on board to make sure that all passengers get ashore, and as a result burns to death. The last four lines convey Hay's message about obligation and sacrifice: "He seen his duty, a dead-sure thing,—/ And went for it thar and then; / And Christ ain't a-going to be too hard / On a man that died for men."[21]

Martí's interest in this piece doubtless lay in the example of heroism and sacrifice, for surely the colloquial language was not of primary appeal. In Hay's poem an "ordinary" man gives his life for others and in so doing gains grace in the eyes of God. Martí's lifelong dedication to a patriotic mission and his willingness to die for a just cause parallel the values expressed in the poem. The selection also highlights Martí's preference for literature of conscience and commitment.

Bret Harte

Bret Harte appears little in Martí's writing. Covering the authors' benefit for the copyright cause, Martí wrote: "Missing from the lecture platform is Bret Harte who from England writes fine and deeply felt stories of the California miners" (11:368). This was the extent of Martí's comment. Although he referred to Harte's stories about California life, he did not name any of the works such as "The Luck of Roaring Camp" or "The Outcasts of Poker Flat" that had made the author famous.

Edward Eggleston

Like a great many other authors, Edward Eggleston had only a cameo appearance in Martí's writing. Martí commented on Eggleston in his 1887 articles for *La Nación* and *El Partido Liberal* about the copyright benefit. For readers in Buenos Aires, Martí depicted Eggleston as a minor man of letters, a producer of Indian biographies, stories from the new states, and commercial works—a writer of everyday topics in fancy binding (11:360). For the Mexican newspaper Martí's report was similar. Eggleston was a writer of task-work who turned out Indian biographies, stories of guides and schools and all sorts of commercial products on comfortable topics and in luxury editions (11:369).

Will Carleton

Will Carleton was identified in Martí's writing as an author of the West. In articles for *El Partido Liberal* and *La Nación*, Martí named Carleton along with John Hay as an author who conveyed the language, style, romance, and daring of the American West (11:260). An 1889 letter for *La Nación* provided further comment on Carleton. Martí was telling about the addition of new states to the Union and described frontier life in the new communities. A home was likely to have "an organ in the corner and a ballad by Carleton and a Bible on the table" (12:262). Martí may have intended this as an allusion to Carleton's *Farm Ballads,* but he did not mention the work by name.

Frank R. Stockton

Frank R. Stockton received slight treatment from Martí: his name appears in only three of the chronicles about American life. A June 1887 letter published in *La Nación* alluded to Stockton's growing fame as a novelist (11:196). Martí's report for *La Nación* about the copyright benefit described Stockton as a "subtle narrator who is now in vogue" and referred to the writer's slight build, saying that Stockton weighed only one hundred twenty pounds—less than what his books weighed (11:360–61). Comments in the same vein were sent in a report to the *Partido Liberal* (11:369–70).

Sidney Lanier

Martí made only three references to Sidney Lanier. His letter to Gonzalo de Quesada of April 1895 listed Lanier as one of the poets included in his writing about the United States (20:478). In a January 1884 article for *La América,* Martí declared that since Sidney Lanier had died, there was really no poet left in the United States except for Walt Whitman (8:428).

Martí's one substantive comment on Lanier was carried in the "Sección Constante" of *La Opinión Nacional* on November 5, 1881. "One of the most notable of the nation's poets, the noble and laborious Sidney Lanier, has died. With him perishes a legitimate hope," Martí wrote. "The cantata that inaugurated the Philadelphia Exposition is his and assured him fame—a fame augmented this last year by the publication of his useful book about English and American men of letters: *The Science of English Verse.* He was benevolent, cultured, and delicate. He died of consumption" (23:63).

Martí's appreciation of Lanier was well-founded. The Georgia poet was one of the most promising figures of the postbellum period, and works Martí mentioned were important contributions. The 1876 cantata, *The Centennial Meditation of Columbia,* featured music by Dudley Buck and lyrics by Sidney Lanier.[22] *The Science of English Verse* revealed Lanier's belief in the relation of music to poetry.[23]

Martí referred to Lanier in his "literary testament"—the letter sent to

Gonzalo de Quesada—and yet wrote little about him. *The Centennial Meditation of Columbia* is one of the poems in the *Patriotic Reader,* a book that was part of Martí's personal library in English, but there is no way of knowing if Martí actually read or studied the piece.[24]

Edward Everett Hale

Edward Everett Hale played a minor role in Martí's theatre of literary figures, and the Cuban writer made no mention of well-known tales such as "The Man Without a Country" and "My Double and How He Undid Me." Readers of Martí's accounts would have learned little about this author from the passing references offered in *El Partido Liberal* and *La Nación.*

In Martí's detailed description of the centennial of Washington's inauguration, sent to the Mexican paper in 1889, he reported that despite the festivities, booksellers had sold no additional copies of the Washington biographies by Hale and Irving (13:503–4). The allusion was to Hale's *Life of George Washington Studied Anew.*

In a December 1889 article for the Buenos Aires public, Martí wrote that the Nationalist Party, which included a respectable group of clergymen, novelists, and philanthropists, was lobbying for social reforms and a change in the industrial order. Then Martí noted with irony that when such claims came from immigrant or foreign voices, the calls for change were deemed dangerous, but when such challenge was expressed by Howells, Hale, or Bellamy, the ideas seemed safe (12:365).

Edward Bellamy

Martí portrayed Edward Bellamy as a reformer. An 1889 article for *La Nación* listed him, along with Hale and Howells, as one of the "respectable" individuals advocating a full reform of the industrial order (12:365). An 1890 letter for the same paper alluded to *Looking Backward* and its treatment of private versus public capitalism but did not name the work (12:427). Martí's chronicle reported on a conflict over the cost and regulation of trains in Texas and raised questions of state versus private control of the railways. In the context of this discussion Martí wrote: "All Texas is carrying Bellamy's book and reading the chapter that tells what railroads will be like in one hundred years . . . when men can get on and

off trains without paying just as they move freely on and off of streets"
(12:427).[25]

Henry James

Martí first mentioned Henry James when he wrote to the editor of *La
Nación* to discuss the coverage he would give to American life. He said
that although Emerson and Longfellow had died and Whittier and
Holmes were but a step from death, America still had a young French-
ified novelist named Henry James (9:18). After this auspicious beginning, however, James virtually disappeared from Martí's texts. Martí
made a summary allusion to James, as a fine worker, in an 1887 piece for
La Nación (6:197), and included a reference in his notes, but that was all.
In the notes Martí listed the works *Confidence, A Bundle of Letters,* and
Washington Square and said of the author: "He writes very correct English in London. He satirizes the provincial ways and worries of Americans with a polished and refined style" (21:135).

James was not as prominent a writer in the United States of the 1880s
as he is today, and most of his important works came after Martí had
essentially ceased to write about American life. Further, James was not
the kind of author with whom Martí would readily identify. James chose
to live disassociated from his native land, believed in the writing of fiction as an art, and constructed works of realism with careful technique.

George William Curtis

George William Curtis shone brightly from Martí's pages as an accomplished public speaker and as a writer and editor who embodied the best
in public life. Martí's initial references were brief: in 1882 he made two
allusions to Curtis as an orator for the columns of *La Opinión Nacional*
(23:212, 13:230). The Cuban writer's appreciation blossomed, however, as
Curtis was linked to the abolitionist cause and calls for political reform.

Events in 1884 prompted a fresh and highly positive perspective on
Curtis. After the noted orator and abolitionist Wendell Phillips died on
February 2, Curtis gave a eulogy at the behest of the municipal authorities of Boston and in a sense spoke for the nation about one of its leading
men.[26] As reader of U.S. life for Spanish Americans, Martí felt called to a

similar task, and in February 1884 he wrote stirring appraisals about Phillips for *La América* and *La Nación*. Martí seemed particularly pleased that his assessment of Wendell Phillips corresponded precisely to Curtis's tribute to Phillips and intimated that the American critic had written him a letter expressing similar sentiments (13:55).[27] In a May follow-up to his *La América* article, Martí noted with pride the parallel characterizations and wrote an enthusiastic endorsement of Curtis (13:55).

Martí's precise portrait of George W. Curtis for the pages of *La América* was framed by their mutual admiration for Wendell Phillips. When Martí waxed eloquent about Phillips, the words touched Curtis as well: "An orator shines through his words but his legacy depends on his deeds" (13:55). Martí wrote that Curtis was famous for "chiseled style, sound judgment, language unafraid of images, and a puritanical rectitude that shines all the more brightly because there are so few left who have it" (12:55). According to Martí, "The United States has no orator more cultured and elegant than he, and for that reason they chose him to give the funeral eulogy for Wendell Phillips. And he gave it in a manner all his own: in style a model, in spirit compassionate, and in judgment even-handed. His eulogy should stand as the nation's definitive statement about the life of the formidable abolitionist" (13:55).

Curtis, an editor at both *Harper's Monthly* and *Harper's Weekly*, was one of the host of writers mentioned by Martí in conjunction with the copyright benefit of 1887. Martí highlighted Curtis's role as a critic and said his words cut furrows through the earth to sow seed (11:360, 369).

Later references took on a more political cast. In April 1888 Martí wrote an article about Roscoe Conkling for *La Nación* and described the implacable rival of James G. Blaine as an arrogant man who dismissed anyone who disagreed with him. Martí said this was true even when an opponent spoke from a position of higher moral ground. To illustrate, he mentioned a comment made by Conkling to Curtis, whom Martí characterized as "an honorable reformer who spoke in gold and wrote in silver" (13:180). According to Martí, Conkling was known for sprinkling his speech with sayings from literature and discourse and had quipped to Curtis that "Johnson was right in declaring patriotism the last refuge of a scoundrel" (13:180). Martí, with a perceptive grasp of the American political scene, understood the irony of Roscoe Conkling's misplaced sarcasm. The words proffered to Curtis were pretentious coming from Conkling; in fact, Curtis had pronounced those words himself in an 1881 paper calling for civil service reform.[28] Martí's contrast of Conkling and Curtis underscored his distaste for presumptuous politicians and his respect for men of integrity (13:180).

Martí in an 1889 article for *La Nación* discussed a Friends of the Negro convention in New York to which Curtis sent words of greeting. Martí again noted Curtis as the eulogist for abolitionist and orator Wendell Phillips (12:337). In another letter for *La Nación,* written a month later, Martí introduced Curtis as an accomplished orator who had voiced disgust with fellow Republicans because the party born to preserve the union was now rotting with the abuses of the spoils system. Martí identified Curtis as an orator of the abolition movement and a father of the Republican Party, who was separating from the Republicans because of opposition to the nomination of James G. Blaine for the presidency. Martí, who deplored Blaine's politics, praised this position and the sense of honor that did not allow Curtis to sit at table with Republican rascals (12:349). For Martí, Curtis's anti-Blaine proclamation in the pages of *Harper's Weekly* was like a banner of stars lighting the political night (12:349).[29]

A February 1890 comment on Curtis described him as an elegant critic and contributor to *Harper's Weekly* whose reputation was beyond reproach. In this context Martí recorded Curtis's honorable reaction to a banking scandal that shone a spotlight on financial fraud and highlighted extradition issues. He translated for his readers Curtis's comment in the February 8 *Harper's Weekly* about a treaty between the United States and Great Britain (12:387–88): "There is always satisfaction in contemplating international acts which are, what they ought to be, frank and simple and without ulterior aims."[30]

Finally, Martí quoted from Curtis in his notes: "—'We only know that however supreme and resistless the genius of a man be, it does not absolve him from the moral obligation that binds us all. / —'Nor is there any baser prostitution than that which would grace self-indulgence with an immortal name.' / (address of George Wm. Curtis, after the unveiling of the statue of Burns at Central Park)" (21:246).[31]

Curtis had qualities Martí admired: principle in politics, sculpted yet sincere writing, gentility, and a golden voice. Martí extolled Curtis's merit and praised his disaffection with political opportunists. Furthermore, it is likely that Curtis was the only notable American author with whom Martí exchanged correspondence.

Charles Dudley Warner

Martí's writing about Charles Dudley Warner falls into three categories: references to Warner's appearance at the authors' copyright reading, reaction to a travel account that Warner wrote for *Harper's* magazine, and unpublished material in notes and correspondence. Of these, comment on Warner's journal about travel to Mexico is by far the most significant.

The comments Martí sent to *La Nación* and *El Partido Liberal* about the 1887 copyright reading included Warner as one of the authors present. Both articles described Warner as the poet of "gardens and solitudes" (11:360, 369). In Martí's notes the Warner entry is simply "(Algo de) [Something by] Dudley Warner" listed underneath the names Thoreau and Borroughs [*sic*] (21:397).

Warner rose to high relief in Martí's survey of American writing only in connection with his 1887 travelogue on Mexico. Martí's reaction was mostly negative, and he registered his chagrin in articles sent to Mexico and Argentina. His comment for *El Partido Liberal* appeared in an article about Mexican presence in the United States; his abbreviated focus on Warner for *La Nación* formed part of a report on the Americas. For Mexican readers, Martí began with a general introduction: "Charles Dudley Warner, the renowned and picturesque writer, describes his journey through Toluca, Pátzcuaro, and Morelia, in unflattering fashion in the pages of *Harper's Magazine*" (7:51). Then the full extent of Martí's irritation boiled over as he dissected Warner's "superficial and pretentious" journey. Martí acknowledged that Warner had the artistic gifts to do justice to Mexico's beauty and that he shared with Thoreau and Burroughs an appreciation of nature. Warner lacked, however, the capacity to capture details with affection and to go beyond mere appearances in taking the measure of a people and a country (7:54–55).

Warner's perspective, not unlike that of many other English and American travel writers of his day, was deeply rooted in notions of linguistic, racial, and cultural superiority. His writing about Mexico extolled the country's natural beauty but betrayed a marked condescension toward her people and traditions—a viewpoint that Martí synthesized precisely: "He understands changes in nature but he cannot understand people of another color" (7:55). A modern reader feeling Warner's disdain for Mexico would probably react with more disgust than Martí's to the American's offensive characterizations and overbearing outlook.

Martí's criticism of the Warner travelogue developed along several lines. When Warner wrote of banditry in Mexico without mentioning the economic conditions that created a climate of need, Martí countered that the United States had experienced similar problems: "And what about the enormous fraud perpetrated by the cultured classes at the pinnacle of U.S. society? Did their abuses not reveal a more vast and inexcusable form of corruption—from which Mexico was virtually free—than occasional acts of robbery?" (7:55). Martí also critiqued Warner's ingenuous description of courtship customs in Mexico, his mistranslation of "calzada" [causeway, walkway] as "shade-place," his ignorance about the situation of Indians in his own country, and his lack of historical background (7:56–57).

Nothing, however, produced a more spirited response on Martí's part than Warner's derision of the results of miscegenation, which ended: "and most notable of all, [are] the dandies of the city, slender-legged, effeminate young milksops, the fag-end of a decayed civilization, without virility or purpose."[32] After conveying the derogatory sentiments in Spanish for his readers, Martí challenged the insult and then admonished: "As if strong legs were the basis for sturdy hearts!" (7:57).

Martí continued with a history lesson for the American author and the following declarations: "Bandy-legged fellows! [The very thought!] Legions of Davids have done more than Goliaths; Simón Bolívar weighed nearly as much as his sword; Miguel Hidalgo [author of Mexican independence] was barely one hundred thirty pounds; bandy-legged men upheld Mexico's honor on the fifth of May. Bandy-legged weaklings indeed!" (7:57).

Martí's other references to Warner figured in letters to his Mexican friend Manuel Mercado. In August 1887 correspondence he lamented not having seen a copy of El Partido Liberal since the one with his letter about the "malevolent" Warner, pardonable only for the fervor with which he described Morelia (20:110). In February 1889 Martí wrote that he had envied Warner ever since the American's travels to Michoacán (22:137).

John Burroughs

John Burroughs appeared chiefly in Martí's notes. In one entry Martí listed him along with Dudley Warner and Thoreau (21:397). Another read: "John Burroughs, más ingenuo, amable y expansivo que Thoreau" [John Burroughs, more open, affable, and expansive than Thoreau] (21: 282). Still another gave a fragment of several sentences in Spanish followed by the name John Burroughs. The passage does not appear to be from Burroughs's works but certainly reflects his thinking and perhaps was written about him. It described someone cultivating his own garden, discovering analogies, learning from nature's variety, and learning about tolerance from nature's peacefulness. It also suggested that the careful observer might know more than a scholar. The closing line was "Many men know about Homer, but not about squirrels" (22:39).[33]

Martí mentioned the naturalist twice in his articles. In writing about Charles Dudley Warner's Mexico journal, Martí said that Warner, like Thoreau and Burroughs, had an appreciation for nature (7:54–55). An August 1890 chronicle for *La Nación* said that if one were going to the countryside to see flowers, he should take along books by Burroughs (12:434). Martí clearly identified Burroughs as a nature writer and regarded him positively but did little to put his name before Spanish American readers.

American realism appealed to Martí largely for the social messages conveyed by its writers. Many of his comments on authors of this group came in the later years of his life in the United States—at a time when he was increasingly focused on planning and promoting the Cuban revolution and less concerned with offering a portrait of American life. Martí's notes and correspondence provide some of the most telling comments about authors of realism. With the exceptions of Helen Hunt Jackson and Mark Twain, he had less interest in these authors than in the romantics and did less to make them known in Spanish America.

Reading America

Martí's knowledge of and experience with U.S. authors affected his life, his political perspective, and his writing. He took solace from Emerson, hope from Twain, and encouragement from the works of Jackson, Hay, Curtis, and others. A primarily positive engagement with U.S. letters helped to temper his largely negative perspective on American politics: he contrasted Emerson with Blaine and Curtis with Conkling, and viewed *A Connecticut Yankee* and *Ramona* as antidotes to the monopolistic tendencies and imperialistic behavior of the colossus. Martí's own work shows the influence of Emerson and is marked by the many voices of American authors who appeared in his translations.

American writers inspired Martí, suggested ideas, and reconfirmed beliefs. Emerson quite likely introduced Martí to the concept of constant ascension to a higher form within nature, and certainly Emerson's life as a man of letters was a model for the Cuban author. Emerson was a kindred spirit who helped Martí appreciate how much nature could teach man and how literary men may see the truth sooner than men of science. Jackson and Miller gave examples of U.S. respect for and concern over Native Americans. Thoreau shared Martí's distaste for academic pomp and pedantry. Twain's Yankee hero gave hope to the beleaguered planner of the Cuban revolution. And Hay's "Jim Bludso" offered an example of courage and sacrifice for others.

Martí's knowledge of nineteenth-century American literary life was substantial, and his coverage was comprehensive. His comments in the essay on Walt Whitman proclaim that one could not know a country without knowing its literature. References, allusions, quotations, translations, and comments related to American writers permeate Martí's work, especially between 1880 and 1895, and provide the leavening that he promised to his editor at *La Nación*. He mentioned at least forty authors and listed more than a hundred titles in U.S. literature.

Martí's reading of American literature brought a broad segment of the nation's literary life to the attention of Spanish Americans, and he was important in introducing Emerson, Whitman, Longfellow, Twain, and Jackson to the Spanish-speaking world. Today, Martí's importance as a transnational figure and his role as cultural icon give renewed importance to the literary links he created in the Americas.

Martí's preferences were reflected in the degree of attention he gave to the various authors. Emerson was first, Whitman and Helen Hunt Jackson of high rank, and Longfellow, the Alcotts, Twain, and Curtis of significance. He wrote of Lowell, Poe, Whittier, and Howells, in part because of their visibility in news and notices of the era. Martí connected Curtis, Howells, and Warner to *Harper's New Monthly Magazine*, where Curtis wrote the "Editor's Easy Chair" section, Howells produced the "Editor's Study," and Warner handled the "Editor's Drawer." Although Martí initially promised to write about James and mentioned Lanier in his literary testament, he said relatively little about either one.

Martí was not only insistent in sharing his knowledge of U.S. authors, he was adamant about the importance of New World literature. These run as dual themes throughout his writing, both public and private. Comments made in the article on Whitman, criticism of a Frenchman's superficial treatment of American letters, and reference to a shipment of books sent to the queen of Italy to prove the existence of "native" American writing are all examples of the importance Martí ascribed to authors in the United States. Martí associated Emerson, Whitman, Longfellow, and Irving with the themes and literature of a new continent and lauded their contributions to cultural autonomy.

Martí's many connections to American literature provide a window on his precepts of literary criticism and a guide to his aesthetic preferences. His declarations in regard to Mark Twain's 1884 lecture in New York are telling. First he stated that people who attended literary events were the ones who promoted ethics in politics and maintained the nation's honor; then he said that the purpose of literature was not to strut like a peacock with showy plumage but to help mankind (10:134–35). While he could praise the way Longfellow softened the sounds of English, find consolation in America's tribute to Whittier, and render adequate translations from Poe, none of these authors fit Martí's profile for excellence in literature. Tears and suffering were the links to authors he respected. Wings were essential to lift an author's spirit, and blood—either touching the wings of inspiration or beating visibly beneath the surface—was necessary for art. In Martí's eyes no anemic author could be successful.

Martí was quick to express appreciation for authors who espoused concern for social justice, acceptance of cultural and linguistic diversity, and respect for the sovereignty of neighboring nations. Thus, he praised Emerson's universality, applauded Longfellow's knowledge of other languages, and endorsed the perceived challenges to American society in Twain's *Connecticut Yankee*. Martí championed Stowe and Jackson as voices of conscience and wrote with approval when Howells condemned imperialistic and anti-immigrant sentiment and Curtis criticized political abuse. Whittier and Bryant gained favor in Martí's eyes with their abolitionist poems and Curtis with his eulogy for the abolitionist Wendell Phillips. Shared sympathies were not enough, however, to earn an author Martí's unrestrained admiration, and Howells was a case in point. Martí acknowledged the American author's honorable social ideals but did not regard him highly as a novelist.

In writing of the literary men and women of the nineteenth century in the United States, Martí remarked upon style and technique as well as beliefs and ideas. He observed that Mark Twain heaped adjectives on a character and made him seem real, that Emerson leaped from thought to thought, that Whitman wrote in the massive strophes appropriate to a growing land, that Whittier composed mother-of-pearl verse, and that Irving's sketches seemed pale and refined when compared to Whitman's energy.

Humor was not of great interest to Martí, especially humor linked to a distinct culture. Except for a passing reference to James Whitcomb Riley's ability to produce laughter—as a public speaker—he expressed very little sympathy for the comedic element in literature. When he did write with approval of humor, it was of laughter designed to serve a moral purpose, such as Locke's satires on the South or Twain's humor in *A Connecticut Yankee*.

Originality impressed Martí even if the author was not a favorite or did not write in Martí's manner. He praised Whitman's vigorous originality although he found it startling at times; he appreciated Poe's novelty while distancing himself from the American's gothic scenes; and he applauded Irving's discovery of sources for literature in the new hemisphere. Martí also liked the freshness and individuality of Mark Twain, who was Martí's opposite in many ways.

Virtuous living impressed Martí, and he praised exemplars such as Emerson, Alcott, and Curtis. He particularly appreciated the writers clustered in the Boston-Concord area—Emerson, Longfellow, the Alcotts, and Thoreau—seeing in them a respect for nature as well as a love of mankind.

An antipathy for professional literary critics joined Martí to Emerson, Lowell, Longfellow, and Howells. Martí noted remarks from these authors suggesting that a professional critic often criticized without contributing constructively himself. Martí's 1882 letter to *La Nación* indicated his own feeling on the matter: since applause was the best indication of praise, silence was the best register of disapproval (9:16).

Some periods of Martí's coverage of American literature were more intense than others. Many authors had been mentioned by 1882, but most local color writers were not named until 1887. Emerson appeared in virtually every phase of Martí's works, while Longfellow was treated principally in the early correspondence. The years 1887 and 1888 were especially important: in those two years Martí wrote the essays on Whitman, the Alcotts, and Whittier, translated *Ramona,* and reported on the copyright reading with its host of writers.

Martí's role as a translator of nineteenth-century American literature has not been fully acknowledged. In addition to his published translations, such as "Fable" by Emerson and Jackson's *Ramona,* his notebooks include fragments and partial translations—some of which are not labeled. His version of Emerson's "Blight," for example, was not recognized as a translation until 1973. We have tended to think that his only translations of poetry are those labeled as such or written in obvious verse form, forgetting that he included Spanish versions of poems within his prose writing: Whittier's "Valuation" and verses from Helen Hunt Jackson and John Howard Payne. Martí also translated and paraphrased nearly seventy lines from Whitman's poetry within the context of a prose essay. He translated poetry from Emerson, Longfellow, Whitman, Poe, Whittier, Jackson, and Payne, and prose from Emerson, Louisa May Alcott, Thoreau, Lowell, Warner, and Curtis.

As an interpreter of American life and literature in the nineteenth century, Martí was essentially sui generis. He commented on many authors, and he was discriminating as a critic, commentator, and translator.

Unlike Sarmiento, Martí saw the rough edges in U.S. learning and letters. Unlike de Tocqueville, he created a thorough and discerning picture of American life. Unlike Rodó, he knew and appreciated the literary legacy of the United States. He had seen its spiritual dimensions expressed in verse and translated Lowell's powerful statement about the value of letters to a nation.

Martí's writing on American authors offers insights about his own reading and his sources. He quoted from magazines and often reported on what the American press had to say about literature. In many instances he appeared to have hastily rendered in Spanish an array of news items garnered from various sources. Martí took this material, seasoned it with his own comments, and then served it to readers in his own style.

In undertaking the enormous task of presenting American literature, Martí faced deadlines, struggled with questions of language and nuance, and sometimes made mistakes. The apostolic mantle bestowed by many Cubans has often made him seem superhuman. Yet his hurried commentary and the occasional mistranslation give his portrait a very human and believable dimension and make his reading of nineteenth-century American letters realistic as well as remarkable.

Notes

Author's note: All citations from Martí, unless otherwise indicated, are from the 28-volume *Obras Completas*. References to this work are given in the text by volume and page number. All translations, unless otherwise indicated, are mine.

Chapter 1. The Making of a Martyr

1. *Versos sencillos* has conventionally been translated as *Simple Verses*, even though "sencillo" is not the equivalent of "simple." Such a translation offers an easy way out of a difficult translating task. However, it betrays the essence of the work: the poems are complex in ways that belie a rubric such as "simple." One way to express the meaning would be to say that the poems represent the sincere songs of an honest heart and convey nature and sentiment without affectation. It is virtually impossible to translate the title effectively in just two words.

2. "Nuestra América" is the title of one of Martí's most famous essays, one that reflects his thinking about Latin America, the ties between the Latin American nations and the United States, and the importance of hemispheric independence—both political and cultural—from Europe. It is frequently anthologized. It was published in both a Mexican newspaper (*El Partido Liberal*) and a New York journal (*La Revista Ilustrada*) in January of 1891.

3. Three recent books give thorough treatment to Martí's relation to *modernismo* and modernity. See *Re-Reading José Martí (1853–1895)*, edited and introduced by Julio Rodríguez-Luis; *Divergent Modernities* by Julio Ramos; and Martí, *Selected Writings*, with an introduction by Roberto González Echevarría. In addition, see Carlos Ripoll's excellent website www.eddosrios.org for comments about Martí's style.

Chapter 2. Life in the United States

1. The French aristocrat Alexis de Tocqueville traveled in the United States in 1831–32 and published the two volumes of his *Democracy in America* in 1835 and 1840. Domingo F. Sarmiento, president of Argentina from 1868 to 1874, was a visitor to the United States in the 1840s, and greatly admired educational models in the United States.

2. One of Martí's most famous lines—"Viví en el monstruo y le conozco las entrañas" [I have lived in the beast and I know her ways] (4:168)—confirms Martí's own assessment of the efficacy of his gaze.

3. John M. Kirk's *José Martí, Mentor of the Cuban Nation*, gives a full analysis of Martí's disillusionment with the United States.

4. The Pan-American Conference of 1889 produced great anguish in Martí. He describes his reaction vividly in the prologue to *Versos sencillos*. For an English translation and explanation of the prologue, see Fountain, *Versos Sencillos by José Martí*, 23–24.

5. Martí's response to the offending editorial was written in English and published by the *New York Evening Post* on March 21, 1889. The piece is known as Martí's "Vindication of Cuba" (1:236–41).

6. Martí's comment in Spanish, written in 1892 in a letter to Pedro Gómez y García, is: "¿Quién por huir de un espantapájaros, se echará en un horno encendido?" (4:425).

7. Baralt, *El Martí que yo conocí*, 43.

8. Two principal sources of information about Martí in New York are Guillermo de Zéndegui, *Ámbito de Martí*, and *Atlas Histórico Biográfico José Martí*.

9. Carlos Ripoll's website www.eddosrios.org offers a comprehensive listing of the New York addresses found in Martí's notes. This list indicates the wide range of New York locales with which Martí was familiar.

10. For an explanation of how Martí's verses have become popular worldwide through the music of Guajira Guantanamera, see Fountain, *Versos Sencillos by José Martí*, 16–18.

11. Gonzalo de Quesada, Martí's disciple, described this effort: "His labor as a correspondent for South and Central American newspapers is a complete review of all the contemporaneous events in the United States. These articles, when collected into a book, will form one of the most profound, entertaining, and just studies of this country" (Quesada and Northrop, *The War in Cuba*, 519).

12. Martí sustained a debate in the press with two newspapers in Mexico that voiced Spanish interests, *La Colonia Española* and *La Iberia*. When these two newspapers claimed that Cubans in the United States had taken no significant part in the American centennial celebrations of 1876 and that they had not participated as a "political entity," Martí refuted the claim with documentation from the American press (1:135–40).

13. The first of Martí's "Impressions of America" was published on July 10, 1880, the second on August 21, 1880, and the last one on October 23, 1880 (19:106–26).

14. The exact number of articles Martí contributed to the *Sun* is subject to debate. See, on Carlos Ripoll's website www.eddosrios.org, "Seis crónicas inéditas" for a complete discussion of the issue.

15. Martí's account of the Cleveland nuptials and of the press frenzy to get details about the bride-to-be is informative not only about the political scene but also about media mania over the private life of a president.

16. Henry George, Edison, Roscoe Conkling, Wendell Phillips, Thomas A. Hendricks, General Hancock, General Sheridan, Henry Ward Beecher, Peter Cooper, Courtlandt Palmer, and Chauncey Depew are examples of well-known men who figured in Martí's writing.

17. Although Martí described at length the ceremonies surrounding the Statue of Liberty, his comments predate the lines by Emma Lazarus inscribed at its base in 1903: "Give me your tired, your poor, / Your huddled masses yearning to breathe free, / The wretched refuse of your teeming shore, / Send these, the homeless, tempest-tossed, to me: / I lift my lamp beside the golden door."

18. Martí lived as he wrote in regard to race relations. He wholeheartedly supported the educational aims and endeavors of black Cubans in New York, and on visits to Tampa he stayed with a black couple, Paulina and Ruperto Pedroso. Martí's essay "Mi raza" (My Race), published in the patriotic journal *Patria* in April of 1893, is a good summation of his thinking on this topic (2:298–300).

Chapter 3. Martí and American Authors

1. A notation in the *Complete Works* states that the chronicle seems to refer to Martí's travel to Mexico in 1875 and 1877 (19:13). The travel diary itself mentions the boat that Martí took from England to New York (19:6).

2. Martí, *The America of José Martí*, 247.

3. The novel is now often referred to as *Lucía Jerez*.

4. "No Successful Substitute for Justice."

5. Ibid.

6. Two recent works have done much to shed light on Martí as a translator. *Martí, traductor* by Leonel Antonio de la Cuesta gives a complete review of Martí's work as a translator. *El traductor Martí* by Lourdes Arencibia Rodríguez provides a more conceptual approach to the topic. Each volume also discusses translation theories and methods as they apply to Martí.

Chapter 4. Martí and Emerson

1. See Martí, *The America of José Martí*, 216–38, and *Martí on the U.S.A.*, 40–52.

2. Schulman, *Símbolo y color*, 58, 150–62.

3. Fountain, "José Martí and North American Authors," 55–56.

4. Martí's affinity for Emerson has been noted by many critics. See Shuler, "José Martí: Su crítica," 175.

5. "I become a transparent eyeball; I am nothing; I see all; the currents of the Universal Being circulate through me; I am part or parcel of God" (Emerson, *Complete Works*, 1:10).

Author's note: Where Martí translates or paraphrases an author, I do not retranslate but give Martí's Spanish in the text, with the author's original in an endnote to allow readers to make their own comparisons of the texts.

6. "What is a farm but a mute gospel?" (Emerson, 1:42).

7. "Give me health and a day, and I will make the pomp of emperors ridiculous. The dawn is my Assyria; the sunset and moon-rise my Paphos" (Emerson, 1:17).

8. See Emerson, 1:11.

9. "This view, which admonishes me where the sources of wisdom and power lie, and points to virtue as to 'The golden key / Which opes the palace of eternity,' carries upon its face the highest certificate of truth, because it animates me to create my own world through the purification of my soul" (Emerson, 1:64; embedded quote from Milton, *Comus*, 13–14).

10. "But is there no intent of an analogy between man's life and the seasons?" (Emerson, 1:28).

11. See Emerson, 1:66–69.

12. "Not only resemblances exist in things whose analogy is obvious, as when we detect the type of the human hand in the flipper of the fossil saurus" (Emerson, 1:43).

13. See Emerson, 1:24.

14. "Thus is Art a nature passed through the alembic of man" (Emerson, 1:24).

15. See Emerson, 1:36–41.

16. "One might think the atmosphere was made transparent with this design, to give man, in the heavenly bodies, the perpetual presence of the sublime.... But every night come out these envoys of beauty" (Emerson, 1:7).

17. "In the woods is perpetual youth. . . . In the woods we return to reason and faith" (Emerson, 1:9–10).

18. "In Haydn's oratorios, the notes present to the imagination not only motions, as of the snake, the stag, and the elephant, but colors also; as the green grass. The law of harmonic sounds reappears in the harmonic colors. The granite is differenced in its laws only by the more or less of heat from the river that wears it away" (Emerson, 1:43–44).

19. See Emerson, 1:26–27.

20. "[M]an is hereby apprized that whilst the work is a spectacle, something in himself is stable" (Emerson, 1:51).

21. See Emerson, 1:36.

22. "The ruin or the blank that we see when we look at nature, is in our own eye. The axis of vision is not coincident with the axis of things, and so they appear not transparent but opaque" (Emerson, 1:73).

23. "Every universal truth which we express in words, implies or supposes every other truth. *Omne verum vero consonat*. It is like a great circle on a sphere, comprising all possible circles; which, however, may be drawn and comprise it in like manner. Every such truth is the absolute Ens seen from one side. But it has innumerable sides" (Emerson, 1:44).

24. "To a man laboring under calamity, the heat of his own fire hath sadness in it" (Emerson, 1:11).

25. "We are not built like a ship to be tossed, but like a house to stand" (Emerson, 1:48).

26. "Leonidas and his three hundred martyrs consume one day in dying" (Emerson, 1:20).

27. "All the facts in natural history taken by themselves, have no value, but are barren, like a single sex" (Emerson, 1:28).

28. Martí, *The America of José Martí*, 237–38.

29. Martí, *Martí on the U.S.A.*, 52.

30. Ibid., 206.

31. "Another striking poem is the 'Boston Hymn,' written for the Day of Emancipation. The overthrow of slavery was a gigantic fact—an event of greater importance than any in our history; and the poet has celebrated it in stanzas rough and impressive as Stonehenge" (Underwood, "Ralph Waldo Emerson," 497).

32. In at least one instance Martí alluded to this struggle in the context of a discussion of Emerson. Martí had commented on the writer Max O'Rell's lack of familiarity with Emerson's poetry, and he continued by noting that O'Rell, along with other writers, had failed to understand that "the free life, in a continent where all the beauties and changes of nature must contend with all the types of the human race, must create an expression worthy of the intense contest in which eagles and worms struggle together" (12:163).

33. From Emerson, 6:84:

Still, through her motes and masses, draw

Electric thrills and ties of Law,

Which bind the strengths of Nature wild

To the conscience of a child.

34. The chapters listed in the volume *The Conduct of Life* are "Fate," "Power," "Wealth," "Culture," "Behavior," "Worship," "Considerations by the Way," "Beauty," and "Illusions"; see Emerson, vol. 6.

35. "Meantime within man is the soul of the whole; the wise silence; the universal beauty, to which every part and particle is equally related; the eternal O-NE" (Emerson, 2:269).

36. "To be great is to be misunderstood" (Emerson, 2:58).

37. "Cut these words, and they would bleed" (Emerson, 4:168).

38. F. Carpenter, *Emerson Handbook*, 51–54.

39. From "Concord Hymn": "Here once embattled farmers stood / And fired the shot heard round the world" (Emerson, 9:158).

40. From "Expostulation": "Slaves, slaves are breathing in that air / Which old De Kalb and Sumter drank!" (Whittier, *Complete Poetical Works*, Riverside ed., 267).

41. From "Under the Old Elm": "Virginia gave us this imperial man" (Lowell, *Complete Writings*, 13:96).

42. Emerson, 11:542.

43. Emerson, 11:297.

44. Emerson, 3:196.

45. Emerson, 8:37.

46. Shuler, "José Martí: Su crítica," 176.

47. Fountain, "Ralph Waldo Emerson and Helen Hunt Jackson," 47–49.

48. Fountain, "José Martí and North American Authors," 87.

49. Rafael Pombo, a Colombian poet and contemporary of Martí, translated the same poem but in a completely different style. In Pombo's translation the rhyme was *abab* throughout and the poem came out to thirty-two lines. Pombo did not convey the meaning or spirit of the poem nearly so well as Martí, and a comparison of the two versions serves to underscore Martí's ability in translating poetry. See Rafael Pombo, *Fábulas y verdades*, 39–40.

50. Emerson, 9:75.

51. Quesada y Miranda, *Facetas de Martí*, 19. In English: "No boundaries bind my heart / I belong to every land: / I am art among art, / A peak among peaks I stand" (Fountain, *Versos Sencillos by José Martí*, 27). Uva de Aragón calls Emerson's reflection in Martí the "pantheism of Emerson" being crystallized in the last two verses of this stanza; see *El caimán ante el espejo*, 94.

52. Ballón, *Autonomía cultural americana*, 39–40.

53. Fountain, *Versos Sencillos by José Martí*, 85.

54. González, *José Martí: Epic Chronicler*, 15–l6 .

55. Shuler, "José Martí: Su crítica," 177–78.

56. Lizaso, "Emerson visto por Martí," 35.

57. Ballón, *Autonomía cultural americana*, 15–33.

58. Schulman, *Símbolo y color*, 47, 53.

59. Ibid., 51–52.

60. Ibid., 56.

61. Ibid., 395–98.

62. Mañach, "Fundamentación del pensamiento martiano," 449.

63. Jorrín, *Martí y la filosofía*, 13.

Chapter 5. Martí and Whitman

1. Sommer, "José Martí, Author of Walt Whitman," 77, and Mir, *Ayer menos cuatro*, 810.

2. For the translations of this essay by Juan de Onís, Luis A. Baralt, and Esther Allen, see Martí, *The America of José Martí*, 216–38, *Martí on the U.S.A.*, 40–52, and *Selected Writings*, 183–94. Gay Wilson Allen's *Walt Whitman Abroad* also has a translation, as does Jaén, *Homage to Walt Whitman*, 55–72.

3. "I announce natural persons to arise" ("So Long!" from *Songs of Parting*, in Whitman, *Leaves of Grass*, 380).

Author's note: All quotations from Whitman that correspond to Martí's references are from the 1881 (seventh) edition of *Leaves of Grass*, since it was the "suppressed" text Martí mentioned in the article and since Martí made a clear reference to this edition elsewhere in his notes. Hereafter *Leaves of Grass* is abbreviated *LG*, followed by the page number; for poems with numbered sections, such as "Song of Myself," the section number is also given.

4. "I harbor for good or bad, I permit to speak at every hazard, / Nature without check with original energy" ("Song of Myself" 1, *LG*, 29).

5. "I announce myriads of youths, beautiful, gigantic, sweetblooded" ("So Long!" from *Songs of Parting*, *LG*, 381).

6. "The smallest sprout shows there is really no death" ("Song of Myself" 6, *LG*, 34).

7. "Knowing the perfect fitness and equanimity of things, while they discuss I am silent, and go bathe and admire myself" ("Song of Myself" 3, *LG*, 31).

8. "I do not say these things for a dollar or to fill up the time while I wait for a boat" ("Song of Myself" 47, *LG*, 75).

9. "I am satisfied—I see, dance, laugh, sing" ("Song of Myself" 3, *LG*, 31).

10. "I have no chair, no church, no philosophy" ("Song of Myself" 46, *LG*, 73).

11. "Oxen that rattle the yoke and chain or halt in the leafy shade, what is that you express in your eyes? / It seems to me more than all the print I have read in my life" ("Song of Myself" 13, *LG*, 38).

12. "To the cotton-field drudge or cleaner of privies I lean, / On his right cheek I put the family kiss" ("Song of Myself" 40, *LG*, 66).

13. Affectionate mentions of Manhattan are frequent in Whitman's poetry.

14. "Superb-faced Manhattan!" and "When million-footed Manhattan unpent descends to her pavements" ("A Broadway Pageant" from *Birds of Passage*, *LG*, 194, 193).

15. "But I will sing you a song of what I behold Libertad" (ibid.).

16. "The institution of the dear love of comrades" ("I Hear It Was Charged Against Me" from *Calamus*, *LG*, 107).

17. Basically a paraphrase of almost the entire poem "City of Orgies" from *Calamus*, *LG*, 105.

18. "I announce myriads of youths, beautiful, gigantic, sweetblooded, / I announce a race of splendid and savage old men" ("So Long!" from *Songs of Parting*, *LG*, 381); "the loud laugh of work-people at their meals" ("Song of Myself" 26, *LG*, 51); "The flap of the curtain'd litter, a sick man inside borne to the hospital, / . . . / What exclamations of women taken suddenly who hurry home and give birth to babes" ("Song of Myself" 8, *LG*, 35).

19. "O powerful western fallen star!" ("When Lilacs Last in the Dooryard Bloom'd" 2, from *Memories of President Lincoln*, *LG*, 255).

20. The idea of death as a harvest is present in Whitman's poetry on Lincoln. The rest of the quote appears to be from the lines "O Death, (for Life has served its turn,) / Opener and usher to the heavenly mansion" ("Gods" from *By the Roadside*, *LG*, 213).

21. "And do not call the tortoise unworthy because she is not something else"; "Oxen that rattle the yoke and chain"; "My tread scares the wood-drake and wood-duck"; "I believe in those wing'd purposes" ("Song of Myself" 13, *LG*, 38).

22. "Has anyone supposed it lucky to be born? / I hasten to inform him or her it is just as lucky to die, and I know it" ("Song of Myself" 7, *LG*, 34).

23. "(No array of terms can say how much I am at peace about God and about death.)" ("Song of Myself" 48, *LG*, 76).

24. "I laugh at what you call dissolution, / And I know the amplitude of time" ("Song of Myself" 20, *LG*, 45).

25. "Whoever degrades another degrades me, / And whatever is done or said returns at last to me. // Through me the afflatus surging and surging, through me the current and index" ("Song of Myself" 24, *LG*, 48).

26. "And as to you Corpse, I think you are good manure, but that does not offend me, / I smell the white roses sweet-scented and growing, / I reach to the leafy lips, I reach to the polish'd breasts of melons" ("Song of Myself" 49, *LG*, 77).

27. "They do not sweat and whine about their condition, / . . . / Not one kneels to another, nor to his kind that lived thousands of years ago" ("Song of Myself" 32, *LG*, 54).

28. "We have had ducking and deprecating about enough" ("Song of Myself" 21, *LG*, 45).

29. "Of every hue and caste am I, of every rank and religion" ("Song of Myself" 16, *LG*, 42).

30. "Let the physician and the priest go home. // I seize the descending man and raise him with resistless will, / O despairer, here is my neck, / By God, you shall not go down! hang your whole weight upon me" ("Song of Myself" 40, *LG*, 66).

31. "Lover divine and perfect comrade" ("Gods" from *By the Roadside, LG*, 213).

32. Perhaps an adaptation of the lines "Through me forbidden voices, / Voices of sexes and lusts, voices veil'd and I remove the veil, / Voices indecent by me clarified and transfigur'd" ("Song of Myself" 24, *LG*, 48).

33. This idea is expressed in "Singing the song of procreation" ("From Pent-up Aching Rivers" from *Children of Adam, LG*, 79) and also in "The oath of procreation I have sworn, my Adamic and fresh daughters" ("Spontaneous Me" from *Children of Adam, LG*, 91).

34. "I sing the body electric" ("I Sing the Body Electric" 1, from *Children of Adam, LG*, 81).

35. "Women sit or move to and fro, some old, some young, / The young are beautiful—but the old are more beautiful than the young" ("Beautiful Women" from *By the Roadside, LG*, 217).

36. "I see the sleeping babe nestling the breast of its mother, / The sleeping mother and babe—hush'd, I study them long and long" ("Mother and Babe" from *By the Roadside, LG*, 217).

37. "Dash me with amorous wet, I can repay you" ("Song of Myself" 22, *LG*, 46).

38. "Divine am I inside and out, and I make holy whatever I touch or am touch'd from" ("Song of Myself" 24, *LG*, 49).

39. "Walt Whitman, a kosmos, of Manhattan the son, / Turbulent, fleshy, sensual, eating, drinking and breeding, / No sentimentalist, no stander above men and women or apart from them" ("Song of Myself" 24, *LG*, 48).

40. "This is thy hour O Soul, thy free flight into the wordless, / Away from books,

away from art, the day erased, the lesson done, / Thee fully forth emerging, silent, gazing, pondering the themes thou lovest best, / Night, sleep, death and the stars" ("A Clear Midnight" from *From Noon to Starry Night, LG*, 369).

41. "O to die advancing on!" ("Pioneers! O Pioneers!" from *Birds of Passage, LG*, 184).

42. "And that night while all was still I heard the waters roll slowly continually up the shores, / . . . / For the one I love most lay sleeping by me under the same cover in the cool night, / In the stillness in the autumn moonbeams his face was inclined toward me" ("When I Heard at the Close of the Day" from *Calamus, LG*, 103).

43. This idea is expressed many times in Whitman's works, but perhaps here is an adaptation of the lines "I am enamour'd of growing out-doors, / Of men that live among cattle or taste of the ocean or woods, / Of the builders and steerers of ships and the wielders of axes and mauls, and the drivers of horses, / I can eat and sleep with them week in and week out" ("Song of Myself" 14, *LG*, 39) and "The dried grass of the harvest-time loads the slow-drawn wagon, / . . . / I am there, I help, I came stretch'd atop of the load" ("Song of Myself" 9, *LG*, 35).

44. "The negro holds firmly the reins of his four horses, the block swags underneath on its tied-over chain, / The negro that drives the long dray of the stone-yard, steady and tall he stands pois'd on one leg on the string-piece, / . . . / His glance is calm and commanding, he tosses the slouch of his hat away from his forehead, / The sun falls on his crispy hair and mustache, falls on the black of his polish'd and perfect limbs" ("Song of Myself" 13, *LG*, 38).

45. "Blacksmiths with grimed and hairy chests environ the anvil, / . . . / From the cinder-strew'd threshold I follow their movements, / . . . / Overhand the hammers swing, overhand so slow, overhand so sure, / They do not hasten, each man hits in his place" ("Song of Myself" 12, *LG*, 37).

46. "The runaway slave came to my house and stopt outside, / . . . / Through the swung half-door of the kitchen I saw him limpsy and weak, / And brought water and fill'd a tub for his sweated body and bruis'd feet, / . . . / I had him sit next to me at table, my fire-lock lean'd in the corner" ("Song of Myself" 10, *LG*, 36). The very last part of Martí's description is a departure from Whitman's text. Martí may have felt that it represented Whitman's feeling, even if it was not part of the poem.

47. "Not asking the sky to come down to my good will" ("Song of Myself" 14, *LG*, 39).

48. "Gentlemen, to you the first honors always! / Your facts are useful, and yet they are not my dwelling, / I but enter by them to an area of my dwelling" ("Song of Myself" 23, *LG*, 47).

49. "How beggarly appear arguments before the defiant deed!" ("Song of the Broad-Axe" 6, from *Children of Adam, LG*, 153).

50. "Lo! keen-eyed towering science, / . . . / Yet again, lo! the soul, above all science" ("Song of the Universal" 2, from *Birds of Passage, LG*, 181).

51. "He that by me spreads a wider breast than my own proves the width of my own." ("Song of Myself" 47, *LG*, 74).

52. "I tramp a perpetual journey, (come listen all!) / My signs are a rain-proof coat, good shoes, and a staff cut from the woods" ("Song of Myself" 46, *LG*, 73).

53. "The dirt receding before my prophetical screams" ("Song of Myself" 25, *LG*, 50).

54. "To conclude, I announce what comes after me." ("So Long!" from *Songs of Parting*, *LG*, 380).

55. "Earth! you seem to look for something at my hands, / Say, old top-knot, what do you want?" ("Song of Myself" 40, *LG*, 65).

56. "I sound my barbaric yawp over the roofs of the world" ("Song of Myself" 52, *LG*, 78).

57. "Remember my words, as I may again return, / I love you, I depart from materials, / I am as one disembodied, triumphant, dead" ("So Long!" from *Songs of Parting*, *LG*, 382).

58. Martí, *Martí on the U.S.A.*, 15.

59. Shuler, "José Martí: Su crítica," 167–72.

60. See Portuondo, *José Martí, crítico literario*, 57–59.

61. Darío published a poem titled "Walt Whitman" in his book *Azul* in 1888. See Alegría's *Walt Whitman en Hispanoamérica*, 24–25.

Chapter 6. Martí and Longfellow

1. José Martí, *Obras Completas: Edición Crítica*, 4:134. This new edition of Martí's works includes information not available in the 28-volume edition. In the references to Longfellow's works, Martí gave abbreviated titles for *The Song of Hiawatha* and *Evangeline: A Tale of Acadie*.

2. See Martí, *Obras Completas: Edición Crítica*, 4:191.

3. This reference is not dated, but Félix Lizaso says in *Martí, Martyr of Cuban Independence*, 256, that on April 15, 1877, Martí announced that he would publish the *Guatemalan Review*.

4. Iduarte, *Martí, escritor*, 55.

5. Austin, *Henry Wadsworth Longfellow*, 198–206.

6. Louis Untermeyer's introduction to *The Poems of Henry Wadsworth Longfellow* has a similar thought: "He was one of the first American poets to break the new earth and make it easier for those who followed to cultivate the rich soil" (xvi).

7. C. Williams, *Henry Wadsworth Longfellow*, 92–93.

8. Martí, *Martí on the U.S.A.*, 38.

9. George Lowell Austin states in *Henry Wadsworth Longfellow*, 295–96, that the clock in the Longfellow home was not the clock described in the poem "The Old Clock on the Stairs," though many people, seeing an old clock on the stairs there, formed that erroneous impression.

10. Longfellow, *Poems*, 41.

11. Description of Pau-Puk-Keewis from *The Song of Hiawatha*: "He was dressed in shirt of doeskin, / White and soft, and fringed with ermine, / All inwrought with

beads of wampum; / He was dressed in deer-skin leggings, / . . . / On his head were plumes of swan's down" (Longfellow, *Works*, 2:194).

12. Translation from Fountain, *Versos Sencillos by José Martí*, 109.

13. Longfellow, *Works*, 7:407.

14. Ibid., 7:330.

Chapter 7. Martí and Writers of the Romantic Movement

1. Irving's five-volume *Life of Washington*, completed in 1859, was considered one of the best biographies of Washington available. Edward Everett Hale also wrote a biography of Washington.

2. Taylor, *Poetical Works*, 350.

3. Probably an allusion to Parke Godwin's 1883 biography of Bryant. Godwin was Bryant's son-in-law and wrote a particularly sympathetic biography.

4. The books in English that were part of Martí's personal library are housed in the José Martí Collection of the Cuban Council of State (Fondo José Martí depositado en Oficina de Asuntos Históricos, Consejo de Estado) in Havana. See Carrington, *Patriotic Reader*, 345–46.

5. Adkins, *Fitz-Greene Halleck*, 158–60.

6. For a complete comparison of Martí's version and the verses from "Home, Sweet Home!" see Fountain, "José Martí and North American Authors," 154–55.

7. Ibid., 157–58, includes a full discussion of the contrast of authors.

8. See Englekirk, *Edgar Allan Poe in Hispanic Literature*, 39.

9. See Schulman, "José Martí y *La Revista Ilustrada de Nueva York*."

10. Englekirk, *Edgar Allan Poe in Hispanic Literature*, 36.

11. de la Cuesta, *Martí, traductor*, 157–63.

12. Arencibia Rodríguez, *El traductor Martí*, 107–14.

13. Ibid., 95–104.

14. Shuler, "José Martí: Su crítica," 174.

15. Moore, *Paul Hamilton Hayne*, 21.

16. The actual name of the poem is "Yorktown Centennial Lyric" (ibid., 124).

17. See "Authors Have a Matinee," 5.

18. Bowen, *Centennial Celebration*, 365.

19. Thoreau, *Writings*, 1:197.

20. Ibid., 11:4.

21. The fir balsam pillow was a gift from the Hampton Institute, at Hampton, Virginia, and gave special pleasure to Mr. Whittier. See "Whittier's Four Score Year," 6.

22. Ibid.

23. Martí's line says, "No sé que el oro os sobre" (23:143), Whittier's "You have less of this world to resign"; see *The Complete Poetical Works of Whittier* (Cambridge ed.), 126.

24. Whittier, *Complete Poetical Works* (Riverside ed.), 126.

25. Ibid., 468.

26. Ibid., 261.

27. Martí's copy of *The Complete Poetical Works of John Greenleaf Whittier* (Cambridge ed.) is housed in the Fondo José Martí (José Martí collection of the Cuban Council of State). I examined Martí's edition of Whittier's poetry on January 15, 2002. It has no notations and thus no indications of what Martí might have read. It does contain the poem "Valuation."

28. Hawthorne, "The Salem of Hawthorne," 3.

29. Ibid., 9.

30. Greenslet, *James Russell Lowell,* 55–56.

31. Lowell, *Complete Writings,* 13:96.

32. From "Our Literature," ibid., 7:276.

33. "Modern Languages," 4.

34. Lowell, *Complete Writings,* 7:308.

35. Ibid., 7:198. These lines are from "Harvard Anniversary," an address given November 8, 1886.

36. Ibid., 12:87. In Lowell's original there are four more lines, separating the first three lines reproduced by Martí from the last two.

37. Holmes, *Writings,* 1:19.

38. Mañach, *Martí, el apóstol,* 27.

39. Adams, *Harriet Beecher Stowe,* 124–27.

40. For a complete comparison of Alcott's writing and Martí's translation, see Fountain, "José Martí and North American Authors," 193–95.

Chapter 8. Martí and Writers of Realism

1. Twain, *A Tramp Abroad,* 54–55.

2. Twain, *Complete Travel Books,* 1:415–16.

3. Martí may have written "Jim," thinking of the scene in chapter 39, "The Yankee's Fight with the Knights," where a voice calls out to the Yankee, "Go it, slim Jim!"; see Twain, *A Connecticut Yankee,* 353.

4. Schulman, "José Martí and Mark Twain," 111.

5. Ibid., 108–9.

6. Ibid., 104.

7. Howells's plea for clemency jeopardized his job with *Harper's* and his standing as a writer; see Kirk and Kirk, *William Dean Howells,* 109–10.

8. Howells, *Poems,* 201–22.

9. Howells, "Editor's Study."

10. Smith, *Mark Twain's Fable of Progress,* 76–82.

11. Rodríguez Morell, "Razones para una metodología," 136.

12. Arencibia Rodríguez, *El traductor Martí,* 55.

13. Jackson, *Poems,* 37.

14. Ibid., 24–25.

15. Fountain, "Ralph Waldo Emerson and Helen Hunt Jackson," 47–49.

16. Martí, 24:204 and 7:54–56.

17. Davis and Alderson, *The True Story of "Ramona,"* 81.

18. Fountain, "José Martí and North American Authors," 220.

19. DeLyser, "Through Ramona's Country," 59.

20. "Hearing the Authors Read," 5.

21. Hay, *Complete Poetical Works,* 5.

22. Parks, *Sidney Lanier,* 31–32.

23. Ibid., 95–99.

24. Carrington, *Patriotic Reader,* 511.

25. *Looking Backward* has no chapter on railroads as such. Martí may have been thinking of Bellamy's Nationalist Party platform, which called for nationalization of the railroads; see Morgan, *Edward Bellamy,* 258–59.

26. Curtis, *Orations and Addresses,* 3:269.

27. Martí said in his message to *La América* that "this gentleman tells us in a kind letter: 'I am very pleased to see that your assessment of the great orator does not differ at all from mine'" (13:55).

28. Curtis's exact words were: "Old professional politicians, who look upon reform as Dr. Johnson defined patriotism, as the last refuge of a scoundrel, either laughed at what they called the politics of idiocy and the moon, or sneered bitterly that reformers were cheap hypocrites who wanted other people's places and lamented other people's sins" (*Orations and Addresses,* 2:173).

29. See, for example, "Important Republican Conventions."

30. "An Admirable Treaty."

31. Curtis, *Orations and Addresses,* 3:307–8.

32. Warner, "Mexican Notes IV—Morelia and Patzcuaro," 287.

33. Martí's entry read: "... cultivando una parte de su jardín propio, descubriendo por sí mismo analogías, aprendiendo lo uno de lo vario, aprendiendo la tolerancia en la paz de la Naturaleza.—Lo que se ve, cuando se observa cuán ignorantes son generalmente los sabios. Muchos hombres saben de Homero, y no de ardillas" (22:39). I found no equivalent for these lines in Burroughs's *Complete Writings.*

Bibliography

Adams, John R. *Harriet Beecher Stowe*. Twayne's United States Authors Series, no. 42. New York: Twayne, 1963.

Adkins, Nelson Frederick. *Fitz-Greene Halleck: An Early Knickerbocker Wit and Poet*. New Haven: Yale University Press, 1930.

Agramonte, Roberto D. *Martí y su concepción del mundo*. Rio Piedras, Puerto Rico: Editorial Universitaria, 1971.

Alcott, Amos Bronson. *Ralph Waldo Emerson: An Estimate of His Character and Genius in Prose and Verse*. 1888. New York: Haskell House, 1968.

Alcott, Louisa May. *Hospital Sketches*. Edited by Bessie Z. Jones. Cambridge: Harvard University Press, Belknap Press, 1960.

———. *Louisa May Alcott: Her Life, Letters, and Journals*. Edited by Ednah D. Cheney. Boston: Little, Brown, 1900.

Alegría, Fernando. *Walt Whitman en Hispanoamérica*. Mexico: Ediciones Studium, 1954.

———. "The Whitman Myth." *Américas* 6, no. 2 (1954): 9–11, 41–42.

Allen, Gay Wilson. *American Prosody*. 1935. New York: Octagon Books, 1966.

———. *Walt Whitman Abroad*. Syracuse, N.Y.: Syracuse University Press, 1955.

———. *Walt Whitman Handbook*. 1946. New York: Hendricks House, 1962.

"An Admirable Treaty." *Harper's Weekly*, February 8, 1890, 98.

Anthony, Katharine. *Louisa May Alcott*. New York: Alfred A. Knopf, 1938.

Aragón, Uva de. *El caimán ante el espejo: Un ensayo de interpretación de lo cubano*. Miami: Ediciones Universal, 2000.

Arencibia Rodríguez, Lourdes. *El traductor Martí*. Pinar del Río, Cuba: Ediciones Hermanos Loynaz, 2000.

Arias, Salvador. *Un proyecto martiano esencial: La Edad de Oro*. Havana: Centro de Estudios Martianos, 2001.

Atlas Histórico Biográfico José Martí. Havana: Instituto Cubano de Geodesia y Cartografía y Centro de Estudios Martianos, 1983.

Austin, George Lowell. *Henry Wadsworth Longfellow: His Life, His Works, His Friendships*. Boston: Lee and Shepard, 1883.

"Authors Have a Matinee." *New York Times*, November 29, 1887.

Ballón, José. *Autonomía cultural americana: Emerson y Martí.* Madrid: Editorial Pliegos, 1986.

———. "José Martí en Nueva York: Dos hitos de su lectura cultural." In *José Martí y los Estados Unidos,* 55–77. Havana: Centro de Estudios Martianos, 1988.

Baralt, Blanca Z. de. *El Martí que yo conocí.* New York: Las Americas, 1967.

Béguez César, José A. *Martí y el krausismo.* Havana: Compañía Editora de Libros y Folletos, 1944.

Bellamy, Edward. *Looking Backward, 2000–1887.* Boston: Ticknor, 1888.

Bigelow, John. *William Cullen Bryant.* American Men of Letters. Boston: Houghton, Mifflin, 1890.

Bowen, Clarence Winthrop, ed. *The History of the Centennial Celebration of the Inauguration of George Washington as First President of the United States.* New York: D. Appleton, 1892.

Boynton, Henry Walcott. *Bret Harte.* New York: McClure, Phillips, 1903.

Bryant, William Cullen. *The Poetical Works of William Cullen Bryant.* Household edition. New York: D. Appleton, 1906.

Burroughs, John. *The Complete Writings.* Wake-Robin edition. 23 vols. New York: Wm. H. Wise, 1924.

Butcher, Philip. *George W. Cable.* Twayne's United States Authors Series, no. 24. New York: Twayne, 1962.

Cameron, Kenneth Walter. *Emerson among His Contemporaries.* Hartford, Conn.: Transcendental Books, 1967.

Cargill, Oscar. *The Novels of Henry James.* New York: Macmillan, 1961.

Carleton, Will. *Farm Ballads.* New York: Harper and Brothers, 1915.

Carpenter, Frederic Ives. *Emerson Handbook.* New York: Hendricks House, 1953.

Carpenter, George Rice. *John Greenleaf Whittier.* American Men of Letters. Boston: Houghton, Mifflin, 1903.

Carrington, Henry B., comp. *Patriotic Reader; or, Human Liberty Developed.* Philadelphia: J. B. Lippincott, 1888.

Corbitt, Roberta Day. "This Colossal Theatre: The United States Interpreted by José Martí." Ph.D. diss., University of Kentucky, 1955.

Corning, A. Elwood. *Will Carleton: A Biographical Study.* New York: Lamere, 1917.

"Courtlandt Palmer." Obituary. *New York Daily Tribune,* July 24, 1888.

Curtis, George William. *Orations and Addresses of George William Curtis.* 3 vols. New York: Harper and Brothers, 1894.

Davis, Carlyle Channing, and William A. Alderson. *The True Story of "Ramona."* New York: Dodge, 1914.

de la Cuesta, Leonel Antonio. *Martí, traductor.* Introduction by Gastón Barquero. Salamanca: Universidad Pontificia de Salamanca, 1996.

DeLyser, Dydia. "Through Ramona's Country: A Work of Fiction & the Landscape of Southern California." *Ventura County Historical Society Quarterly* 42, nos. 3–4 (1997): 49–63.

Emerson, Ralph Waldo. *Complete Works.* Centenary edition. 12 vols. Boston: Houghton, Mifflin, 1903–4.

Englekirk, John Eugene. *Edgar Allan Poe in Hispanic Literature.* New York: Instituto de las Españas, 1934.

———. "El epistolario Pombo-Longfellow." *Thesaurus* (Bogotá) 10 (1954): 1–58.

———. "Notes on Longfellow in Spanish America." *Hispania* 25, no. 3 (1942): 295–308.

Fatout, Paul. *Mark Twain on the Lecture Circuit.* Bloomington: Indiana University Press, 1960.

Ferguson, John De Lancey. *American Literature in Spain.* New York: Columbia University Press, 1916.

Fernández Retamar, Roberto. *Introducción a José Martí.* Havana: Casa de las Américas, 1978.

———. "Un periodista argentino llamado José Martí." *Universidad de La Habana* 245 (1995): 133–45.

Fondo José Martí depositado en Oficina de Asuntos Históricos, Consejo de Estado de Cuba. (José Martí Collection housed in the Office of Historical Affairs, Cuban Council of State.) Havana.

Fountain, Anne. "José Martí and North American Authors." Ph.D. diss., Columbia University, 1973.

———. "Ralph Waldo Emerson and Helen Hunt Jackson in *La Edad de Oro.*" *SECOLAS Annals* 22 (March 1991): 44–49.

———. *Versos Sencillos by José Martí: A Translation.* University, Miss.: Romance Monographs, 2000.

García Marruz, Fina. "El tiempo en la crónica norteamericana de José Martí." In *Temas Martianos,* 175–89. Havana: Centro de Estudios Martianos, 1995.

———. "Los Versos Sencillos." In *A Cien Años de Martí,* compiled by Tony T. Murphy, 17–50. Las Palmas: Ediciones del Cabildo Insular de Gran Canaria, 1997.

Godwin, Parke. *A Biography of William Cullen Bryant.* 2 vols. New York: Russell and Russell, 1883.

González, Manuel Pedro. *José Martí: Epic Chronicler of the United States in the Eighties.* Chapel Hill: University of North Carolina Press, 1953.

Gray, Richard Butler. *José Martí, Cuban Patriot.* Gainesville: University of Florida Press, 1962.

Greenslet, Ferris. *James Russell Lowell.* American Men of Letters. Boston: Houghton, Mifflin, 1905.

Griffin, Martha I. J. *Frank R. Stockton: A Critical Biography.* Port Washington, N.Y.: Kennikat Press, 1965.

Hale, Edward Everett. *James Russell Lowell and His Friends.* Boston: Houghton, Mifflin, 1899.

Harrison, John M. *The Man Who Made Nasby: David Ross Locke.* Chapel Hill: University of North Carolina Press, 1969.

Hawthorne, Julian. "The Salem of Hawthorne." *Century* 28, no. 1 (1884): 3–17.

Hay, John. *The Complete Poetical Works of John Hay*. Boston: Houghton, Mifflin, 1916.

Hayne, Paul Hamilton. *Poems*. Boston: D. Lothrop, 1882.

"Hearing the Authors Read." *New York Daily Tribune,* November 30, 1887.

Hill, Roscoe R. "Martí, Intérprete de los Estados Unidos de América." In *Memoria del Congreso de Escritores Martianos*. Havana: Comisión Nacional Organizadora de los Actos y Ediciones del Centenario y del Monumento de Martí, 1953.

Holloway, Jean. *Edward Everett Hale*. Austin: University of Texas Press, 1956.

Holmes, Oliver Wendell. *Writings*. Riverside edition. 13 vols. Boston: Houghton, Mifflin, 1891–95.

Horner, George F., and Robert A. Bain, eds. *Colonial and Federalist American Writing*. New York: Odyssey Press, 1966.

Hough, Robert L. *The Quiet Rebel: William Dean Howells as Social Commentator*. Lincoln: University of Nebraska Press, 1959.

Howells, William Dean. *A Chance Acquaintance: A Selected Edition of William Dean Howells*. Edited by Jonathan Thomas and David J. Nordloh. Vol. 6. Bloomington: Indiana University Press, 1971.

———. "Editor's Study." *Harper's New Monthly* 81, no. 483 (1890): 476–81.

———. *Poems*. Boston: Houghton, Mifflin, 1901.

Iduarte, Andrés. *Martí, escritor*. 2d ed. Havana: Publicaciones del Ministerio de Educación, 1951.

"Important Republican Conventions." *Harper's Weekly,* October 5, 1889, 790.

Jackson, Helen Hunt. *Poems*. Boston: Little, Brown, 1898.

———. *Ramona*. Boston: Roberts Brothers, 1884.

Jaén, Didier Tisdel, ed. and trans. *Homage to Walt Whitman: A Collection of Poems from the Spanish*. University: University of Alabama Press, 1969.

Jiménez, Juan Ramón. "José Martí." *Archivo José Martí* 1 (1940): 9–12.

Jorrín, Miguel. *Martí y la filosofía*. Havana: Editorial Hercules, 1954.

Kennedy, William Sloane. *John Greenleaf Whittier: His Life, Genius, and Writings*. New York: Saalfield, 1903.

Kirk, Clara M., and Rudolf Kirk. *William Dean Howells*. Twayne's United States Authors Series, no. 16. New York: Twayne, 1962.

Kirk, John M. *José Martí, Mentor of the Cuban Nation*. Tampa: University Presses of Florida, 1983.

Lasplaces, Alberto. *Vida admirable de José Varela*. 2d ed. Montevideo: Claudio García, 1944.

Lanier, Sidney. *The Centennial Meditation of Columbia: A Cantata for the Inaugural Ceremonies at Philadelphia, May 10, 1876*. New York: G. Schirmer, 1876.

Leary, Lewis. *John Greenleaf Whittier*. Twayne's United States Authors Series, no. 6. New York: Twayne, 1961.

Lizaso, Félix. "Emerson visto por Martí." *Humanismo* (Havana) 3, no. 23 (1954): 31–38.

————. *Martí, Martyr of Cuban Independence.* Translated by Esther Elise Shuler. Albuquerque: University of New Mexico Press, 1953.

————. *Pasión de Martí.* Havana: Ucar y García, 1938.

Long, E. Hudson. *Mark Twain Handbook.* New York: Hendricks House, 1957.

Longfellow, Henry Wadsworth. *The Poems of Henry Wadsworth Longfellow.* Edited by Louis Untermeyer. New York: Heritage Press, 1943.

————. *Works.* Standard Library edition. 14 vols. Boston: Houghton, Mifflin, 1924.

Lowell, James Russell. *Complete Poetical Works.* Cambridge edition. Boston: Houghton, Mifflin, 1924.

————. *Complete Writings.* Elmwood edition. 16 vols. Boston: Houghton, Mifflin, 1904.

Lynn, Kenneth S. *William Dean Howells: An American Life.* New York: Harcourt Brace Jovanovich, 1971.

McElderry, Bruce R., Jr. *Henry James.* Twayne's United States Authors Series, no. 79. New York: Twayne, 1965.

McLean, Albert F., Jr. *William Cullen Bryant.* Twayne's United States Authors Series, no. 59. New York: Twayne, 1964.

Mañach, Jorge. "Fundamentación del pensamiento martiano." In *Antología crítica de José Martí,* edited by Manuel Pedro González, 443–57. Mexico: Editorial Cultura, 1960.

————. *Martí, el apóstol.* 2d ed. Buenos Aires: Espasa Calpe, 1944.

Martí, José. *The America of José Martí.* Translated by Juan de Onís. New York: Noonday Press, 1953.

————. *Escritos desconocidos de José Martí.* Edited by Carlos Ripoll. New York: Eliseo Torres and Sons, 1971.

————. *Martí on the U.S.A.* Translated and introduced by Luis A. Baralt. Carbondale: Southern Illinois University Press, 1966.

————. *Obras Completas.* 28 vols. Havana: Editorial Nacional de Cuba, 1963–73.

————. *Obras Completas: Edición Crítica.* Vol. 4. Havana: Centro de Estudios Martianos, 2001.

————. *Selected Writings.* Edited and translated by Esther Allen. Introduced by Roberto González Echevarría. New York: Penguin, 2002.

————. *Versos.* Edited by Eugenio Florit. New York: Las Americas, 1962.

Martin, Terrence. *Nathaniel Hawthorne.* Twayne's United States Authors Series, no. 75. New York: Twayne, 1965.

Martínez Gómez, Yolanda. "Algunas consideraciones sobre el Martí, crítico." *Archivo José Martí* 17 (1951): 374–80.

Milne, Gordon. *George William Curtis and the Genteel Tradition.* Bloomington: Indiana University Press, 1956.

Mir, Pedro. *Ayer menos cuatro y otras crónicas (1945–1980).* Compiled and with an interview by Francisco Rodríguez de León. Santo Domingo: Biblioteca Nacional de la República Dominicana, 2000.

"Modern Languages." *New York Times,* December 29, 1889.

Monte, Domingo del. *Escritos de Domingo del Monte.* Edited by José A. Fernández de Castro. 2 vols. Havana: Cultural, 1929.

Moore, Rayburn S. *Paul Hamilton Hayne.* Twayne's United States Authors Series, no. 202. New York: Twayne, 1972.

Morgan, Arthur E. *Edward Bellamy.* Columbia Studies in American Culture, no. 15. New York: Columbia University Press, 1944.

Morse, John Torrey, Jr. *Life and Letters of Oliver Wendell Holmes.* 2 vols. Boston: Houghton, Mifflin, 1899.

"No Successful Substitute for Justice." *Century* 35, no. 4 (1888): 650.

Onís, José de. *The United States as Seen by Spanish American Writers, 1776–1890.* New York: Hispanic Institute in the United States, 1952.

Orjuela, Hector H. *Biografía y Bibliografía de Rafael Pombo.* Bogotá: Instituto Caro y Cuervo, 1965.

Parks, Edd Winfield. *Sidney Lanier: The Man, the Poet, the Critic.* Athens: University of Georgia Press, 1968.

Parrington, Vernon Louis. *Main Currents in American Thought.* 3 vols. New York: Harcourt, Brace, 1930.

Peterson, Martin Severin. *Joaquin Miller: Literary Frontiersman.* Stanford: Stanford University Press, 1937.

Piñeyro, Enrique. *Hombres y Glorias de América.* Paris: Garnier Hermanos, 1903.

Poe, Edgar Allan. *Complete Works.* Edited by James A. Harrison. 17 vols. New York: Thomas Y. Crowell, 1902.

Pombo, Rafael. *Fábulas y verdades.* Bogota: Imprenta Nacional, 1916.

———. *Poesías completas.* Madrid: Aguilar, 1957.

Portuondo, José Antonio. *José Martí, crítico literario.* Washington, D.C.: Unión Panamericana, 1953.

Pumar, Pedro. *Ramona (drama-adaptación radio-teatral).* Caracas: Ediciones de La Torre, 1937.

Quesada y Aróstegui, Gonzalo de, and Henry Davenport Northrop. *The War in Cuba.* 1896; reprint, New York: Arno Press, 1970.

Quesada y Miranda, Gonzalo de. *Facetas de Martí.* Havana: Editorial Trópico, 1939.

Rabassa, Gregory. "Walt Whitman visto por José Martí." *La Nueva Democracia* (New York) 39 (1959): 88–93.

Ramos, Julio. *Divergent Modernities: Culture and Politics in Nineteenth-Century Latin America.* Translated by John D. Blanco. Foreword by José David Saldívar. Durham: Duke University Press, 2001.

Randel, William Pierce. *Centennial.* Philadelphia: Chilton, 1969.

———. *Edward Eggleston.* Twayne's United States Authors Series, no. 45. New York: Twayne, 1963.

Revell, Peter. *James Whitcomb Riley.* Twayne's United States Authors Series, no. 159. New York: Twayne, 1970.

Ripoll, Carlos. Website with articles by and about Martí at www.eddosrios.org.

Rodríguez-Luis, Julio, ed. *Re-Reading José Martí (1853–1895): One Hundred Years Later*. Albany: State University of New York Press, 1999.

Rodríguez Morell, Jorge Luis. "Razones para una metodología de análisis de la traducción martiana en *Ramona*." *Anuario del Centro de Estudios Martianos* (Havana) 18 (1995–96): 133–40.

Sarmiento, Domingo Faustino. *Sarmiento's Travels in the United States in 1847*. Translated and introduced by Michael Aaron Rockland. Princeton: Princeton University Press, 1970.

Schulman, Ivan. "José Martí and Mark Twain: A Study of Literary Sponsorship." *Symposium* (Syracuse) 15, no. 2 (1961): 104–13.

———. "José Martí y *La Revista Ilustrada de Nueva York*." *Cuadernos Americanos* 27, no. 4 (1968): 141–53.

———. *Símbolo y color en la obra de José Martí*. 2d ed. Madrid: Editorial Gredos, 1970.

Schulman, Ivan, and Manuel Pedro González. *Martí, Darío y el modernismo*. Madrid: Editorial Gredos, 1970.

Schyberg, Frederik. *Walt Whitman*. Translated by Evie Allison Allen. New York: Columbia University Press, 1951.

Shuler, Esther Elise. "José Martí: Su crítica de algunos autores norteamericanos." *Archivo José Martí* 16 (1950): 164–92.

Slater, Joseph, ed. *The Correspondence of Emerson and Carlyle*. New York: Columbia University Press, 1964.

Small, Miriam Rossiter. *Oliver Wendell Holmes*. Twayne's United States Authors Series, no. 29. New York: Twayne, 1962.

Smith, Henry Nash. *Mark Twain's Fable of Progress: Political and Economic Ideas in "A Connecticut Yankee."* New Brunswick, N.J.: Rutgers University Press, 1964.

Sommer, Doris. "José Martí, Author of Walt Whitman." In *José Martí's "Our America,"* edited by Jeffrey Belnap and Raúl Fernández, 77–90. Durham: Duke University Press, 1998.

Stedman, Edmund Clarence. *Poets of America*. Boston: Houghton, Mifflin, 1895.

Stovall, Floyd, ed. *Eight American Authors*. New York: W. W. Norton, 1963.

Symington, Andrew James. *William Cullen Bryant: A Biographical Sketch*. New York: Harper and Brothers, 1880.

Taylor, Bayard. *Poetical Works*. Boston: Houghton, Mifflin, 1903.

Thoreau, Henry David. *Writings*. Walden edition. 20 vols. Boston: Houghton, Mifflin, 1906.

Twain, Mark. *The Complete Travel Books of Mark Twain*. Edited by Charles Neider. 2 vols. Garden City, N.Y.: Doubleday, 1966–67.

———. *A Connecticut Yankee in King Arthur's Court*. New York: Harper and Brothers, 1889.

———. *The Family Mark Twain*. New York: Harper and Brothers, 1935.

———. *A Tramp Abroad.* 1888. New York: Heritage Press, 1966.

Underwood, Francis Henry. "Ralph Waldo Emerson." *North American Review* 130, no. 282 (1880): 479–98.

Van Doren, Mark. *Nathaniel Hawthorne.* New York: Viking Press, 1962.

Vitier, Medardo. *Martí, estudio integral.* Havana: Comisión Nacional Organizadora de los Actos y Ediciones del Centenario y del Monumento de Martí, 1954.

Wagenknecht, Edward Charles. *William Dean Howells: The Friendly Eye.* New York: Oxford University Press, 1965.

Warner, Charles Dudley. "Mexican Notes IV—Morelia and Patzcuaro." *Harper's New Monthly* 75, no. 446 (July 1887): 283–91.

Whitman, Walt. *The Collected Writings of Walt Whitman.* Comprehensive Reader's edition. Edited by Harold W. Blodgett and Sculley Bradley. New York: New York University Press, 1965.

———. *Leaves of Grass.* Philadelphia: David McKay, 1888 (c. 1881).

Whittier, John Greenleaf. *Complete Poetical Works.* Riverside edition. Boston: Houghton Mifflin, 1894.

———. *The Complete Poetical Works of Whittier.* Cambridge edition. Boston: Houghton, Mifflin, 1894.

———. *Writings.* 7 vols. Boston: Houghton, Mifflin, 1894.

"Whittier's Four Score Year." *New York Daily Tribune,* December 18, 1887.

Williams, Cecil B. *Henry Wadsworth Longfellow.* Twayne's United States Authors Series, no. 68. New York: Twayne, 1964.

Williams, Stanley Thomas. *The Spanish Background of American Literature.* 2 vols. New Haven: Yale University Press, 1955.

Zéndegui, Guillermo de. *Ámbito de Martí.* Madrid: Escuela Gráfica Salesiana, 1954.

Index

Anne Fountain teaches Latin American literature and culture at San José State University. She is the author of *Versos Sencillos by José Martí: A Translation* and specializes in Martí's role as a transnational figure.